MW01281946

the
tanka
anthology

Tanka in English
from Around the World

Edited by
Michael McClintock, Pamela Miller Ness & Jim Kacian
with an Introduction by
Michael McClintock

the tanka anthology
First Publication, 2003
Red Moon Press
PO Box 2461
Winchester VA 22604

ISBN 1-893959-40-6
Printed in the United States of America
First Edition

Dedicated to Sanford Goldstein—
scholar, poet, friend.

The editors proffer special thanks and gratitude to John Barlow, Sanford Goldstein, Laura Maffei and Michael Dylan Welch for their advice, assistance, care and support during the preparation of this book.

Michael McClintock
Pamela Miller Ness
Jim Kacian

Contents

Introduction

POETRY IS MORE THAN A BEAUTIFUL OPIATE. If we seek "to get the news from poems" in that same way William Carlos Williams wrote about in his poem "Asphodel, That Greeny Flower," we will find it here.

This is an anthology of tanka in English, compiled from collections, chapbooks, small journals, and magazines published during the past thirty years. A significant number appear here for the first time. As with most anthologies, however, more poems have been set aside than included. The selection seeks to represent each poet's finest work and to best demonstrate the variety, strengths, and achievements of English-language tanka.

CULTURAL CONTEXT FOR TANKA IN ENGLISH

What today is popularly called "tanka" evolved from the *waka* (Japanese poetry) written by nobles and aristocrats in the Heian court centered at Kyoto during the twelfth century. Like those *waka*, the modern tanka in this anthology reflect the times, locales, places, societies, and lives of the people who wrote them. That essential communication is what claims our interest and attention. They are not imitation tanka but the authentic article. The poets who wrote them live in contemporary cities such as Liverpool, Los Angeles, and Toronto; in small towns and villages in Australia, Scotland, and Wales; on farms and in desert and wilderness regions of four continents. Most of the poets have been writing tanka for a decade, some for twenty years, and a few such as Sanford Goldstein for thirty years or more. Several are new arrivals. A good number have established reputations as haiku poets whose work is read throughout most of the world and appears in W. W. Norton's third edition of Cor van den Heuvel's *The Haiku Anthology* (1999) and other well-known anthologies.

Two great poetry anthologies compiled in the eighth century, the *Kojiki* (712) and the *Man'yoshu* (ca. 759), contain the seed and roots of tanka, and a third and later anthology, the *Kokinshu* (ca. 905), its first flowering. Tanka, a word that means "short poem", is actually a relatively new term, coined in the early 1900s in Japan by *waka* reformers—Yosano Tekkan, Yosano Akiko, Masaoka Shiki, and others. Known as *waka* up until that later period, it was the foremost poetry of Japan for a thousand years and is still hugely popular.

Not surprisingly, interest in the possibilities of tanka in English grew as more and more of this literature was translated and made available in books such as Donald Keene's famous *Anthology of Japanese Literature from the Earliest Era to the Mid-Nineteenth Century* (1955), which includes selections from the *Kojiki*, *Man'yoshu*, and *Kokinshu*, as well as tanka from other sources. Keene's book was widely read and is still on reading lists in colleges and universities. Its popularity established the careers of a number of translators who contributed to it, encouraging them and others to present their work in other books to a curious, hungry public.

Japanese tanka, haiku, senryu, and other forms and genres of Asian poetry received unprecedented exposure during the 1950s and 1960s. Preceding tanka in popularity and interest during this period, haiku was first to be thoroughly quarried, assayed, and brought into English due largely to the work of Harold G. Henderson and R. H. Blyth. Henderson's *The Bamboo Broom* (1934), *An Introduction to Haiku* (1958), and *Haiku in English* (1965) and Blyth's luminescent four-volume *Haiku* (1949-52) provided the foundation for haiku in English. The popularity of other books, among them the Peter Pauper Press books of tanka and haiku and Kenneth Yasuda's *Japanese Haiku* (1957), further accelerated early experimentation with haiku, as did poems written in the haiku manner by Jack Kerouac (later published in *Scattered Poems*, 1971), Gary Snyder, and Allen Ginsberg.

Models for a viable tanka in English came a few years later. Among these, Kenneth Rexroth's *One Hundred Poems from the Japanese* (1964) enjoyed popular success. Though criticized by scholars for inaccuracies and certain liberties, Rexroth's translations read well as poems in English and seemed in tune with the new voice in poetry emerging from the San Francisco Renaissance during that time. Carl Sesar's translation of Ishikawa Takuboku in *Poems to Eat* (1966), and Sanford Goldstein's translations of Akiko Yosano in *Tangled Hair* (1971) and more of Takuboku in *Sad Toys*

(1977), exerted further influence over early efforts to adapt tanka to a contemporary idiom that suspended some rules of grammar and used fragmented syntax.

English literature has always been eclectic in its forms and genres. Imitation and invention characterize a common assimilation process, providing its warp and woof. Adapting and assimilating the songs and poetic forms of other cultures and languages began early and continues into the present day. Tanka is just one of many recent arrivals.

Very few of the forms and poetic modes most used in poetry in the English-speaking world originated with the mother tongue of Chaucer. English verse assimilated its use of harmony, refrain, and fixed rhyme structure from the Italian sonnet, terza rima, and ottava rima. Minstrels and other song-makers happily added the "fixed" or prescribed verse forms of the French jongleurs and troubadours: the rondel, rondeau, triolet, villanelle, and ballade. The sagas of Scandinavia and Iceland lent their alliterative schemes to the Anglo-Saxon scop's word-hoard and the gleeman's recitations. The ancient civilizations of Greece and Rome left a rich legacy wherein the English poets found their fundamental models for the epic, ode, idyll, and lyric. Other poetic modes and forms, such as the epigram, elegy, epistle, monologue, soliloquy, apostrophe, and aphorism, became the-stock-in-trade of English verse. Since first translated into seventeenth century English and published in the King James Bible, the varied, strong cadences of ancient Hebrew have also profoundly influenced and helped mold English-language poetry.

With this mixed pedigree in view, tanka is neither strange nor exotic. Its adaptation and assimilation into English during the past fifty years connects and relates it to a network of various cultural streams, traditions, and poetic types, all of which contribute their texture to the English language where tanka now also makes its home. Tanka has already absorbed the traits and peculiarities of the surrounding culture—in the United States, Canada, and the United Kingdom especially, and at a slower pace in Australia, New Zealand, and elsewhere in the English-speaking world. It will surely continue to do so, becoming different from the tanka of Japan, yet still of the same species.

For over two thousand years the chief interest of the West in the East was economic, ruled by trade. Only in the last century have those interests expanded to thoroughly embrace and encounter the arts, philosophies, religions, and literature of these regions. As new literary translations appeared, an almost religious enthusiasm overcame the old views of Eastern destinations as little more than sources for trade in exotic commodities, fabulous wealth, and profit.

SOME TANKA PRECURSORS

Eclectic patterns and processes accelerated following World War II, bringing into contemporary English-language poetry many of the popular, traditional verse forms and genres of the East. The dominance of free verse and unrhymed, unmetered forms that has characterized much of the poetry of English-speaking regions for the past hundred years helped to create a readiness to explore and adapt where possible the rich, deep, and long literary traditions of Asia. In the United States, this movement has paralleled the nation's emergence from the insularity of its homogenous, Euro-centered, and largely rural culture. Economic trade and political and military conflict have been other factors.

There are also homegrown roots for tanka. Numerous precursors can be found in the poetry of the early twentieth century, especially in the work of the Imagists of the United States and Great Britain. The Imagists' exaltation of a poetry that approached its subject matter directly, unencumbered by superfluous words or rigid, metronomic rhythms, finds an echo in the tanka of this anthology.

This following five-line stanza that concludes William Carlos Williams' short "Love Song," from his first collection *Al Que Quiere!* (1917), looks and feels much like today's tanka in English:

> Who shall hear of us
> in the time to come?
> Let him say there was
> a burst of fragrance
> from black branches.

The interrogative of the first two lines, the stanza's two-part structure, the poem's alliteration, and its vivid, single image from nature are all elements common to traditional Japanese tanka and its English cousin.

Similarly, Ezra Pound's "April" from *Personae* (1926) anticipates much that is found in contemporary tanka:

> Three spirits came to me
> And drew me apart
> To where the olive boughs
> Lay stripped upon the ground:
> Pale carnage beneath bright mist.

The distinctly musical cadence, simple diction, clarity, and intensity typify many of the best tanka in English. Only Pound's accented meter and use of a title remain relatively uncommon in contemporary tanka. Japanese poetic perception and expression, studied by the Imagists, influenced this work.

Another prominent Imagist, H. D. (Hilda Doolittle) occasionally used five-line stanzas in her longer poems that anticipated the irregular cadences, tone, and mood of tanka written in English many decades later. Here are stanzas of three poems in H. D.'s *Heliodora and Other Poems* (1924):

> Keep love and he wings
> with his bow,
> up, mocking us,
> keep love and he taunts us
> and escapes.
>
> —from "Eros, Part III"

I had thought myself frail;
a lamp,
shell, ivory or crust of pearl,
about to fall shattered,
with spent flame.
                    —from "Eros, Part IV"

All Greece hates
the still eyes in the white face,
the luster as of olives
where she stands,
and the white hands.
                    —from "Helen"

In each of these, many features within the five-line structure that anticipate the modern English-language tanka: the asymmetry of short and long lines and, as with Pound, an irregular but distinctly musical cadence, simple diction, clarity of image, and intensity of emotion. Though born in Pennsylvania, H.D. moved to London in 1911 and became one of the Imagist circle in England that included Richard Aldington, T. E. Hulme, F. S. Flint, and Edward Storer. This group retained a fascination with Greek and Roman myth and carried over into the early twentieth century the neo-Classic preoccupations of Matthew Arnold and Algernon Swinburne. In contrast, the American Imagists, such as Amy Lowell, William Carlos Williams, the early Wallace Stevens, and others, tended to look to the East for their inspirations and models. Ezra Pound straddled both interests, producing many fine translations from the Chinese while incorporating Greco-Roman themes, motifs, and figures into other work. Always restless, Pound eventually left the Imagists in quest of new adventures; the movement was fast devolving into what Pound decried as "Amygism" and no longer held his interest.

Adelaide Crapsey is often mentioned in connection to tanka in English. Many have regarded her invention of the five-line cinquain as an attempt to find a formal equivalent to the brevity and lyricism of Japanese tanka. Susan Sutton Smith's introduction to her book *The Complete Poems and Collected Letters of Adelaide Crapsey* (1977) documents Crapsey's exposure to tanka in William N. Porter's *Single Verses by a Hundred People* (1909), a translation of the *Hyaku-nin-isshu*, a collection of *waka* compiled in the thirteenth century by Sadaiye Fujiwara. Sutton also shows that Crapsey evidently studied Michel Revon's *Anthologie de la Littèrature Japonaise des Origines un XXᵉ Siecle* (1910), and Yone Noguchi's *From the Eastern Sea* (1910), containing original poems and translations from the Japanese. It is equally clear from Sutton's book, however, that Crapsey was in fact much more interested in the meters and syllabary of *Paradise Lost*, the longer poems of Tennyson, and nursery rhymes; she wanted to discover the shortest possible form of metrical English verse. Tanka happened to be a rather small digression in the course of Crapsey's efforts. The cinquain she created in her small but remarkable body of about thirty poems was uniquely her own. Here is an example:

Amaze

I know
Not these my hands
And yet I think there was
A woman like me once had hands
Like these.

The notion that Crapsey's cinquain is a purely syllabic verse form persists to this day. In fact, the Crapseian cinquain is rigidly accentual-syllabic, the five lines having a stress pattern of 1, 2, 3, 4, and 1 in a pattern of 2, 4, 6, 8, and 2 syllables, the iambic foot being the key. Crapsey's poems appeared posthumously in *Verse* (1915), a small collection that made her reputation. That same year, Sadakichi Hartmann, who was something of a frenetic character in orbit around various East Coast literary scenes in the United States, saw his chapbook *Tanka and Haikai: 14 Japanese Rhythms* (1915) published by Guido Bruno in New York. During the past thirty years, few poets writing tanka in English have shown much interest in using comparable schemes for accented meter in their verse; clearly, however, Crapsey's cinquain suggests the value that such an approach could have and a direction the tanka might one day take. Interestingly, a significant number of the contributors to *Amaze: The Cinquain Journal,* edited and published on the Web and as a print journal in California by Deborah P. Kolodji, are well-known English-language tanka and haiku poets.

Meanwhile, at the end of the nineteenth century in Japan, work was underway to reform and revitalize the Japanese *waka*. Various groups emerged to challenge the standard poetic diction and strict adherence to conventions that had been enforced by critics for centuries. One such group was the Shasei ("sketch from life") Movement, inspired by Masaoka Shiki's call for tanka reform and the examples of his own verse. Up to the time of his death in 1902 from tuberculosis, Shiki as poet and critic had been busy tossing out tradition-clad styles and language in favor of more contemporary idiom and subject matter. He accomplished the same thing with haiku. Janine Beichman's study, *Masaoka Shiki: His Life and Works* (1982), is an especially worthwhile account of Shiki's work at bringing the revered but toothless tanka and haiku into the modern world. Tanka had stagnated badly during the Medieval (1186-1587) and Tokugawa (1603-1867) periods, as had haiku in the long years following the deaths of Basho, Buson, Issa, and members of their immediate circles. Makoto Ueda's *Modern Japanese Tanka: An Anthology* (1996) offers a broader discussion and survey of the Meiji (1868-1912) and Showa (1926-1989) periods' leading tanka poets, detailing their feverish efforts to resolve the clash of old and new values and to incorporate into their tanka both influences from the West and a revised assessment of tanka tradition.

Even though tanka clearly had a formative influence on the Imagists, as did haiku, as poetic form and genre in its own right tanka was left unexplored and largely unknown until the Beat revolution and renaissance centered in San Francisco and New York City in the 1950s and 1960s. In addition to the titles already mentioned relating specifically to tanka and haiku, a number of other early books on Asian thought and religion helped to pave the way for a renewed, more vigorous, and lasting interest. Important among these are Alan Watts' *The Spirit of Zen* (1935), Witter Bynner's *The Way of Life According to Lao-tzu: An American Version* (1944), and the numerous books by D. T. Suzuki, Lin Yutang, and others. The popularity of these and similar books created receptive audiences not just for the new luminaries of literature and the Beat Generation but also for the serious exploration and assimilation of haiku, tanka, and other forms and genres.

EMERGING INFRASTRUCTURE FOR TANKA IN ENGLISH

While haiku grew popular in the 1960s and 1970s, tanka in English hesitated. In his instant classic *The Haiku Handbook: How to Write, Share, and Teach Haiku* (1985), the meticulous critic, researcher, and translator of haiku, William J. Higginson, devoted a number of pages to a discussion of tanka. For this period, he cites only three original tanka collections in Western languages: Jorge Luis Borges' *The Gold of the Tigers* (1977), Sanford Goldstein's *Gaijin Aesthetics* (1974), and Michael McClintock's *Man With No Face* (1974). The shortness of the list was astonishing. A year after Higginson's book, a few early tanka appeared in Simon and Schuster's second edition of Cor van den Heuvel's *The Haiku Anthology* (1986). In Japan at this time, Machi Tawara's first tanka collection *Sarada Konembi* (*Salad Anniversary*, trans. by Jack Stamm, 1988) was selling millions of copies.

There were at least two reasons for tanka's laggardly pace. One was its lack of visible, effective champions. Lucille M. Nixon was one of the exceptions; until her death in 1963, she avidly promoted tanka to poetry groups and in the small presses throughout the United States. With Tomoe Tana, Nixon also translated *Sounds from the Unknown: A Collection of Japanese-American Tank*a (1963), published by small but prestigious A. Swallow in Denver. The book is a valuable record of work by tanka poets who were virtually unknown outside the Japanese-American community. Another exception has been Benedictine Father Neal Henry Lawrence, who began lecturing about tanka throughout the United States and Japan in the 1960s.

The second and most obvious reason for tanka's slower steps relative to English haiku was the paucity of places where tanka could be published. This situation began slowly to change. One of the earliest publications to regularly welcome tanka in its pages was the curiously titled *Janus & SCTH*. It was a tiny journal edited and assembled by Foster Jewell and his wife Rhoda de Long Jewell in Sangre de Cristo, New Mexico. *Janus & SCTH* mixed sonnet, cinquain, tanka, and haiku into a pleasing format. It flourished through most of the 1960s and into the early 1970s. Regular contributors of tanka included Ruby L. Choy, Eve Smith, William E. Lee,

Jean Saucer, and a tankaist from Israel, Walter M. Barzelay. Jewell himself preferred to make his reputation in haiku, writing many memorable poems that strongly evoked the subtle moods and spaces of New Mexico's deserts and mountains. Many poets still writing today found their first exposure to tanka in *Janus & SCTH*'s pages.

Elsewhere, tanka in English began to appear in other small poetry journals of the day. They were usually titled, or simply labeled "tanka," and printed in the odd, otherwise unfilled space an editor might find available on a page. Most of the work was undistinguished, usually imitative, and now and then plain silly.

Magazines that regularly devoted space to tanka were rare. The main haiku magazines, such as *Modern Haiku, Frogpond*, and *Dragonfly*, did not publish tanka. Tanka only occasionally appeared in *Haiku Magazine* under William J. Higginson, who had taken it over from Eric Amann in Canada and moved it to New Jersey in 1971.

The tempo began to pick up during the late 1980s. Don Wentworth's *Lilliput Review* began publishing short poems of all types in 1989. It has always been friendly toward tanka, especially through the later 1990s, publishing them alongside short poems in other styles by Cid Corman, Albert Huffstickler, Lyn Lifshin, Alan Catlin, and numerous other well-known, prolific poets. Published in Pittsburgh, Pennsylvania, *Lilliput Review* still thrives. *Hummingbird: Magazine of the Short Poem*, published quarterly by Phyllis Walsh in Richland

Center, Wisconsin, reflects a philosophy similar to the *Lilliput Review*, and carries tanka in every issue.

Another important development for tanka in English, also starting up at the end of the 1980s, was Jane Reichhold's Aha! Books and the magazine *Mirrors*, in Gualala, California. Mirrors was mostly a haiku magazine, but almost immediately began to sponsor the annual *Mirrors* International Tanka Awards. Both ventures generated considerable energy and brought English-language tanka poets into contact with tanka poets throughout the world. The momentum created by these efforts was encouraging; Reichhold began a new and expanded magazine in 1995, *Lynx*, and the well-known Tanka Splendor Awards. Both continue to this day, though in 1999 *Lynx* ceased its print publication to become a Web magazine, regularly publishing tanka among a variety of other genres and forms.

Elsewhere on the west coast, also in 1989, the Haiku Poets of Northern California group launched its quarterly magazine *Woodnotes*. Until the mid-1990s, most of the magazine's space was devoted to haiku and senryu; tanka began to appear more frequently in its later years, or from about 1994 to its last issue in 1997. Various editors were involved in the magazine's history. For a time, Christopher Herold and Michael Dylan Welch served as joint-editors; Ebba Story and Kenneth Tanemura served as associate editors at different periods, and Pat Shelley was the magazine's tanka editor during its last year or two of publication. Though *Woodnotes* had a regional flavor, centered in San

Francisco, it was read and widely distributed throughout the United States.

The 1990s saw still more magazines and journals open their pages to tanka. Brian Tasker edited and published *Bare Bones* for a number of years in the United Kingdom. Also in Britain, ai li began publication of *Still* in 1997. *Still* presented tanka, haiku, and other short poetry in an attractive one-poem-per-page, perfect-bound format between beautiful, full-color covers featuring ai li's own photography. The tanka and haiku between the covers were consistently among the most interesting and innovative anywhere. *Still* ceased publication in 2001, after five years.

Another British newcomer in the 1990s is Snapshot Press, an independent poetry publisher specializing in English-language tanka and haiku books and journals. Snapshot publishes the tanka journal *Tangled Hair*, edited by John Barlow, and sponsors in alternating years annual book competitions for unpublished collections of tanka and haiku. The prize-winning collections are published in attractive, perfect-bound editions and distributed worldwide. Upon its launch in 1999, *Tangled Hair* was, and still is, the only non-American journal dedicated solely to tanka in English. Tanka are presented one per page in a perfect-bound, pocketsize format with full-color cover.

Meanwhile, Sanford Goldstein and Kenneth Tanemura published several issues of their brief venture, *Five Lines Down*, and *RAW NerVZ Haiku*, edited by Dorothy Howard, became Canada's leading publication for haiku, tanka, and related poetry and prose. It continues to specialize in poems that regularly test the boundaries of the tanka and other genres.

In the United States, Laura Maffei founded and began editing *American Tanka* in 1996. This was a watershed event. Published twice a year in a perfect-bound edition of more than a hundred pages, with one tanka per page, *American Tanka* quickly became the world's premiere journal for original English-language tanka. With its appearance, tanka in English at last had a publication where the focus was undividedly on tanka, carefully selected, handsomely printed, and regularly issued.

Back on the west coast of the United States, the last issue of *Woodnotes* carried Welch's announcement of his new venture, *Tundra: The Journal of the Short Poem*. From its inception in 1997 to 2003, *Tundra* appeared twice. Handsomely produced and presented, *Tundra* offered a wide-ranging blend of tanka, haiku, and senryu with other short poems, including free verse, cinquain, clerihews and limericks. Also following the demise of *Woodnotes*, the Haiku Poets of Northern California began regular publication of a new membership journal, *Mariposa*. Appearing biannually, *Mariposa* features tanka along with haiku, senryu, and related forms, and is edited by Claire Gallagher and Carolyn Hall.

While *Modern Haiku* and *Frogpond* continue their policy of excluding tanka, the British haiku journals, *Presence*, edited by Martin Lucas, and *Blithe Spirit: The*

Journal of the British Haiku Society, now regularly carry English-language tanka in their pages.

Capping a busy decade, in April of 2000 a group of like-minded people met in Decatur, Illinois to discuss the need for a broad based organization devoted to tanka. Formation of the Tanka Society of America was the result. TSA began publishing a quarterly newsletter that same year under the editorship of Pamela Miller Ness. Michael Dylan Welch served as the organization's first president. Both the organization and its newsletter continue to grow, providing a much-needed nexus for tanka study, discussion, and information. *The TSA Newsletter* regularly publishes essays, articles, translations, reviews, and other information relating to both Japanese and English-language tanka. One of its columns, "Tanka Café", regularly discusses and highlights new tanka by TSA members. Yet an additional activity is the annual TSA International Tanka Contest, conducted each April.

A list of magazines and journals publishing tanka in English follows this introduction. Considering that the December 2, 2002 issue of *The New Yorker* published a tanka by well-known poet Richard Wilbur (and labeled it simply "Tanka") the list is by no means exhaustive. Tanka now appear frequently in dozens of poetry magazines and other periodicals, large and small, throughout the United States, Canada, the United Kingdom, and elsewhere.

Indeed, outside of Japan, tanka are nowhere more robust and popular today than in the English-speaking world.

In form, techniques, and subject matter, the modern English-language tanka shows wide variation and invention and appears disinclined to observe any rigid set of "rules" or conventions.

As might be expected in the early stages of adaptation, English-language tanka poets first imitated the Japanese models and strictly adhered to a 5-7-5-7-7 syllabic structure and pattern of short/long/short/long/long lines deduced from them. Generally, this resulted in poems that were too long in comparison to Japanese tanka or that were padded or chopped to meet the fixed number of syllables. Over time, most tanka poets set aside the 5-7-5-7-7 requirement and explored a more resilient free-verse approach, grappling along the way with the issues of using or not using rhyme, titles, and alternate lineation schemes. The work of the leading translators was assiduously studied. Most of these, such as Makoto Ueda, Stephen D. Carter, Sanford Goldstein, and Laurel Rasplica Rodd rendered their translations in five lines. There were other approaches, however. H. H. Honda advocated the use of the quatrain for tanka; Kenneth Rexroth occasionally used a four-line structure in his renderings of Japanese tanka. Hiroaki Sato continues to favor the one-line format for his translations.

While poets continue to experiment, the contemporary tanka in English may be described as typically an untitled free-verse short poem having anywhere from about twelve to thirty-one syllables arranged in words and phrases over five lines, crafted to stand alone as a unitary, aesthetic whole—a complete poem. Excepting those written in a minimalist style, a tanka is about two breaths in length when read aloud. During the last thirty years, it has emerged as a robust short form that is identifiable as a distinct verse type while being extremely variable in its details.

Other structural features and many of the techniques and subjects of English-language tanka are represented by the examples below; we will refer to each of them in the discussion that follows:

Example 1: flush left, 5-7-5-7-7 formal pattern

a sudden loud noise
all the pigeons of Venice
at once fill the sky
that is how it felt when your hand
accidentally touched mine

Example 2: indented, 5-7-5-7-7 formal pattern

the black negligee
that I bought for your return
hangs in my closet
day by day plums ripen
and are picked clean by birds

Example 3: indented

>a gnat's smudge
>on my forearm—
>>the smallest death
>>i have known this year
>>but typical

Example 4: staggered, 5-7-5-7-7 formal pattern

>ah, summer, summer,
>how quickly you fade. I cut
>>rusted zinnias,
>>place them on a glassed table-
>>top, as if time could double.

Example 5: staggered

>The days I did not sing
>>the nights I did not dance
>>>their joy
>>>>spiraling out of the throat
>>>>of a hermit thrush

Example 6: centered, 5-7-5-7-7 formal pattern

>>>Just out of earshot,
>>>the periodic blinking
>>>of a night airplane,
>>>not quite far enough away
>>>to be as close as the stars

Example 7: minimalist

> Lightning on
> the horizon
> my child
> takes a huge
> bite from a pear

Example 8: tumbling/minimalist

> at the funeral of
> one who said
> God is dead
> God is
> dead

Example 9: free form

> I
> who am not really
>   a cook
> poke gently into
> a green pepper

Example 10: expanded

> centered
>   by north light
> the potter's wheel
>   small dreams
>   within the curve of her hands

For every tanka set aside here for scrutiny, ten others in the anthology might have been chosen to serve the same purpose. Within the five lines, all manner of variation takes place. None of these configurations is rigidly observed; the name I have used for each is meant only to describe the structure and lineation.

Few tanka poets write consistently in a single, unvaried pattern of line arrangement. The alternation of short and long lines frequently varies. While the majority of tanka in English appear with a left-aligned or "flush left" margin, many poets employ indentations, staggered lines, and other spacing variations. These arrange-ments emphasize certain lines, phrases, or single words, or give the poem a sense of movement or shape on the page that is intended to enhance the meaning, tone, or emotion evoked. A few variations appear simply to be matters of the poet's (or editor's) own taste, or purely cosmetic, such as the centering of lines in Example 6.

Other fundamental elements of structure are also at work, creating tension and interplay of form with content. These have to do with cadence, rhythm, accents, or stresses, the use of end-stopped lines or rhetorical line breaks, caesuras within lines and phrases, enjambment, juxtaposition of images, or a pairing of distinct strophe-antistrophe components within the poem. These elements—not the number of syllables in a line—are the decisive elements in tanka structure as written in English. In contrast to Japanese tanka, which mostly use a fixed, prescribed form with a long history of formal conventions relating to mechanics, techniques, and subject matter, tanka in English have relatively few such constraints or requirements in pattern or organization. In English-language tanka, we find intuitive, functional, and organic approaches to form and content that result in a complex but necessary interrelationship of parts; no bodies of "rules" need to be followed to achieve the desired effect of the whole. While informal syntax and the patterns and vocabulary of common speech predominate, these very broad commonalities display remarkable, polychromatic diversity in tone, mood, and expression.

As with many tanka in this set of examples, Example 1, by Ruby Spriggs, reflects traditional tanka subject matter, involving topics of love, sorrow, personal remembrance or introspection, or nature. Often, tanka read like notes from a diary and convey a single event that has some special significance in the poet's life or consciousness—a realization, personal insight, or memory. Spriggs's poem also shows how the basic structural features of Japanese tanka have been adapted. The pattern of short/long/short/long/long lines is intact, and the use of thirty-one syllables in five lines of 5-7-5-7-7 parallels the pattern of thirty-one sound units of Japanese tanka. This is one of the formal patterns tried by many poets for English-language tanka during the early days of experimentation and adaptation; some still use it today, and in the literature it is frequently referred to as "traditional." It results in a poem that is, however, almost twice as long in time duration as a

Japanese tanka, with a good deal more information.

"Venice" won first prize in the traditional category in the First North American Tanka Contest held in 2001. The judge, Professor Jan Walls, author and oriental scholar at Simon Fraser University, commented on how the poem "takes the familiar touristic image of startled pigeons simultaneously taking flight, and unexpectedly relates the cause/effect sequence to a personal romantic incident. The imagery is fresh and startling; the content is powerfully meaningful . . . at the personal level; and the craft is exquisite—it reads like a tanka, but will be immediately appreciated by any English reader who may know nothing about tanka."

Margaret Chula also uses the 5-7-5-7-7 formal pattern in Example 2. Both poems are dramatic and anecdotal, telling a story in few words but with intensity and conviction. However, here indentation is used to emphasize the poem's two component movements. Rather than a personal comment or reflection, Margaret Chula's final two lines offer a stark "objective correlative" to the image and mood of the preceding three lines, encapsulating the poet's thoughts in implicit metaphor. The juxtaposition is surprising, and the despairing realization is made even more powerful by not being named—the bleak image of the ripened plums "picked clean by birds" says it all. Unlike the Spriggs poem, the two images here are not directly compared but set in sharp contrast. The effect approaches, but is not quite, surreal.

William Ramsey's tanka in Example 3 illustrates a

reversal in the basic two-component structure, the couplet element coming first and bearing the poem's single image. The poet's response in the final three lines is made more acerbic by "falling back" to a short, concluding line.

Consider also the movement Geraldine Clinton Little's poem in Example 4. Also a poem of 5-7-5-7-7 syllables, this tanka is more complicated, having three parts and given momentum by the use of enjambment: "ah summer, summer / how quickly you fade" functions as the strophe, "I cut / rusted zinnias, / place them on a table- / top," is the antistrophe, and the poem's sliding to a rest on "as if time could double" functions as a kind of epode. The enjambed strophes and abrupt shifts generate tension and underscore the poet's wistful contemplation of time's evanescence. The reflected double-image of the zinnias on the glass tabletop is an especially powerful image, again showing the use of an objective correlative to convey both idea and emotion while preserving aesthetic distance.

Carol Purington's poem in Example 5 is distinctly lyrical. The parallel construction of the opening two lines is that of a song. The strong accents on the final words in each line move the poem forward with a sense of "lifting". The poem's progression from the general "The days I did not sing" to the specific and beautiful "throat of a hermit thrush" is lilting—almost like a bird in flight. The staggered line arrangement visually assists this sense of movement. If its lines were all aligned left, how different this poem would read!

In Example 6 by Gerald St. Maur, the first three lines could stand alone as a haiku, a feature that may be found in many tanka in this anthology. Such tanka combine the objective imagery of a haiku with a subjective response or personal reflection in the poem's concluding lines; the order can also be reversed. It is the subjective element in a tanka that chiefly distinguishes it from most haiku, in addition to its greater length. Here, the concluding two-line component is a simple, personal reflection or response to the initial image, placing the silent aircraft in the context of a starry sky. The twist in sense here—that the aircraft is the more remote, alien object—gives a postmodern slant to the traditional tanka theme of loneliness.

A feature of many tanka in English is the employment of one of several conceptually related devices or methods that are used to change the direction of the tanka between the first and second components. This transition is often called the "pivot". Sometimes it is achieved simply by juxtaposing two images (Examples 2 and 7), or an image and a response (Example 3), or by the movement from strophe to antistrophe (Examples 1 and 4). At other times the pivot functions like the *volta*, or turn, in a sonnet, where the sense of the poem is momentarily suspended and a new idea introduced—this is what occurs in the line "their joy" in Carol Purington's poem, and in the line "not quite far enough away" in Gerald St. Maur's tanka. Ruby Spriggs accomplishes her pivot with a hemistich or half line: "that is how I felt . . ." Sometimes, too, the pivot in a tanka is achieved by a line that completes the thought or image of the first component, or strophe, and can be read also as the first line of the second component, or antistrophe. In other words, the sense of the line is shared by both components, but changes in meaning or significance from one to the other. The term for this technique is "zeugma". Francine Porad is especially adept in using pivots of this kind. Here is an example, in which "as the train passes" is the shared line:

> a woman
> holds the waving child high
> as the train passes
> where . . . when . . .
> did summer disappear

In such tanka, the strophe and antistrophe are the key units of composition. Some critics appear to think that the presence of a pivot in tanka is essential, taking the Duke Ellington view of rhythm and jazz: "It don't mean a thing if it ain't got that swing." Must all tanka have such a pivot point? Most tanka in English seem to, though it frequently can be so subtle as to go unnoticed. At other times, the pivot is emphatic and surprising. There is, in fact, no requirement for the use of this technique, in English-language or Japanese practice. Its absence does not mean the poem is not a tanka.

Example 7, by Robert Kusch, is a tanka in a more minimalist style. Kusch uses a syntactic pivot: two images are simply juxtaposed, or abutted, without transition or even punctuation. No subjective element or stated interpretation appears; we assume only a temporal contiguity between the two images. The immediacy and effect are very haiku-like and defy paraphrase or elaboration. Such force holds the combined images together so that they fuse into a third image that is stunning, magical, wordless, yet utterly mysterious in meaning or significance. The Japanese have a word for it, *yugen*, meaning sublimity, or mysterious depth.

Another minimalist poem is LeRoy Gorman's droll "at the funeral" in Example 8, a mere fourteen syllables. The structure is Skeltonic, tumbling from six syllables to one, ending emphatically on the word "dead." It is a one breath in length, like a haiku, a trait shared by most minimalist tanka. Unlike haiku, it contains no image. For these reasons, and because of its content, some might argue that the poem is more akin to senryu, haiku's satirical cousin. Many minimalist tanka present this same quandary of classification—would they not be haiku or senryu if written in the conventional three lines of those genres? It is not a problem that will be resolved here; like most minimalist poems, Gorman's poem seems to take an insurgent posture toward any comfortable definition. It represents a crossover tanka, of which there are many in this anthology, most notably by ai li, Fay Aoyagi, Sanford Goldstein, Philip Rowland, Alexis Rotella, and others. They are so numerous, in fact, that perhaps they represent a subgenre of tanka in English.

Many English-language tanka might in fact be regarded by most Japanese as being a subgenre of tanka, known as *kyoka*, or "mad poems," containing satire, sometimes even crudity, with little or no attempt to be lyrical. These poems are sometimes like an epigram, humorous and opinionated, occasionally acerbic and biting. At the other end of the spectrum, they may be playful or light in mood or, like Gorman's, gently mocking in tone. The *kyoka* is to the tanka what senryu is to the haiku. Like senryu, they can be rather sharp, penetrating observations of human faults, foibles, and failings. A confessional quality is present in those where the poet is both observer and observed.

Some of the finest English-language tankaists frequently write in *kyoka* style. Here is one by Laura Maffei:

> energy waning
> as the afternoon wears on
> a grim coworker
> leans into my cubicle
> whispering conspiracy

Such comic portrayals of modern life, often containing social or political commentary, are very much the substance, voice, and character of tanka in English, and represent its departure from the traditional subject matter of Japanese tanka. Leatrice Lifshitz's encounter with a green pepper, in Example 9, is a further illustration. At present, there seems little practical reason to separate these seemingly *kyoka*-like poems and make them a subgenre, or to place them in a class by themselves and call them something else; they are too much a part of what tanka is in English. Values are based on inclusions as much as exclusions.

anne mckay's tanka, in Example 10, represents still another approach to structure, introducing the dimension of space. The words appear to float on the page, invested with light, eddying toward the final image of the potter's hands. This tanka is one of a series by mckay appearing in this anthology that deal with the subject of light, invoked as both physical phenomenon and metaphysical presence. The poem's form accords perfectly with its content and delicate lyricism.

In the foregoing examples, punctuation either is absent or kept to the bare minimum. This is typical of most tanka in English. Only a few poets—Alexis Rotella and Pamela Miller Ness are two—consistently use periods at the end of lineated sentences or at the end of a poem; they also use initial capitals. These features give their tanka a very slight, relative formality. Other poets, such as George Swede and Karina Young, capitalize only the first word of a tanka. Many have used different approaches over the years.

Metrical patterns, or accented metric feet, are certainly possible in the English-language tanka. Such patterns would be meaningless in Japanese, which places a uniform stress on the last syllable of each word. English syllables do not equate to the Japanese sound unit; converting English syllables to Japanese sound units, or vice versa, is not a one-for-one exchange. Some tanka in this collection do, in fact, show deliberate use of accentual meter in their lines, adding to the poem's other dimensions of rhythm, sound, and fluidity when read silently or aloud. In the following tanka by Cherie Hunter Day, the basic metric unit is the iambic foot, one short or unstressed syllable followed by a stressed or long syllable (lines one to four):

> through patterned glass
> see how the water bends
> the flower stems
> my heart and many other
> optical illusions

The iambic rhythm breaks in the fifth line, where a dactyl foot (OP-ti-cal) is followed by an amphibrach foot (il-LU-sions), playfully emphasizing the sense and meaning of the words.

While set rhyme schemes have never been used in tanka, traditional end rhyme and internal rhyme do occasionally occur. Slant and half-rhyme, involving assonance and consonance, appear with greater frequency. These uses of rhyme work in conjunction with alliteration, caesura, and line breaks to emphasize certain words or phrases, to control the pace or cadence in a tanka, to build or release tension, and to help make one movement in a poem distinct from another. Assonance in the last two lines of this tanka by John Barlow conveys a subtle and unusual musicality:

dawn
and you open
your deep-green eyes—
blackbirds stir
somewhere in the conifers

Almost all issues continue to be argued and debated by poets, scholars, and critics. James Kirkup in Andorra argues in favor of a strict adherence to a 5-7-5-7-7 syllabic measure in English. Gerald St. Maur has advocated the use of titles for individual tanka, while others argue that in a poem so brief this is tantamount to adding a sixth line. A compromise might be the occasional use of a simple headnote; in Japan, a headnote often appears with a tanka to provide information pertinent to the poem's composition, such as where it was written, on what occasion or event, or some other detail. However, these headnotes do not function as titles do. Of course, titles are used for tanka collections, sequences or "strings," and other groupings. A tanka sequence by Ruby Spriggs, "After Chemo," is included in this anthology as an example.

While the method and craft of tanka in English varies considerably from the conventional rigors of Japanese practice, clearly both approaches result in verses that manifest and share similar poetic mood and temper. In each, the powers of compression, nuance, implication, and understatement are orchestrated to evoke emotion or describe an image or experience. Variations that do exist reflect differences in culture and language. We can speak of "the tanka spirit" as a quality in the poems that is held broadly in common, in much the same way as haiku poets throughout the world today speak of "the haiku spirit." The tanka of Japan appear to embody intrinsic values of expression and understanding that are robust enough to not only survive but also thrive when transferred to another culture and language.

It may be argued that the differences between Japanese tanka and its English-language counterpart are less important than the intrinsic similarities. They indeed have much in common, but beyond a certain undefined point—one that is perhaps intuited only—differences are certainly to be expected and even encouraged, so that each may take full advantage of the resources of its own language and culture. Tanka in English may deviate within the tanka tradition in order to create their own distinct flavor and build their own integrity, while at the same time preserving the formal and mechanical techniques that are fundamental to all tanka.

TANKA THEMES AND TOPICS

As good as some translations may be, any reading of the *Man'yoshu* or *Kokinshu* indicates that these are songs from another shore, another time. Yet at their core they express universal human emotions. These emotions are easily recognizable, meaningful, familiar, and accessible to the modern reader whose society and life outwardly have little in common with the tanka poets of the Heian, Medieval, or Tokugawa periods in Japan. We read them for the same reasons we still read Chaucer, or Shakespeare, or the gospel of John: They continue to tell us about ourselves and to make the human experience shareable and intrinsically fascinating in its diversity, valued in its commonalities, and available for close inspection.

The tanka exists somewhere in that huge universe between the awareness of death and the sheer joy of life, helping to preserve the balance in each of us as we go about our daily business. Some might say that emotion, not thought, is at the center of tanka. The poetry itself does not seem to support such a sweeping generalization. It seems apparent that tanka is poetry of emotion as well as idea, thought and imagination.

Consider the following tanka by Francine Porad that won first prize in the Poetry Society of Japan's Third International Tanka Contest in 1992:

> Michaelangelo
> tapped his Moses on the knee
> arise and walk!
> I kiss the cherry-red mouth
> on the canvas

Emotion abounds here, certainly. But the poem also has other themes relating to the imagination and intellect, wherein begins the hero's journey toward the "wild surmise" of the mind that Keats knew as well as this Michaelangelo, here brought to such exuberant life. This is a tanka of passion, without doubt, but is it not also a paean to something more than a cherry-red mouth?

Contemporary tanka in English reflect all the themes and most of the subjects found in more than a thousand years of Japanese tanka. Poems of romantic love make up a significant subgenre within contemporary tanka, and just as in Heian times the poems range between extremes, from the playful, silly, and occasionally plain sappy to the obsessive, self-tortured, sultry, and toxic, and appear to be written by a more or less equal number of men and women.

Other aspects of love—love for home, for family, for a spouse, parent, or child, for a pet, for a particular place, for a particular time of day or night or season, for a work of art, even for a particular possession or object—appear throughout tanka literature, now as before. And so also does the entire universe of feelings associated with such themes: loss, triumph, regret, distance, isolation, desire, guilt. Some modern tanka in English could have been written five hundred or a thousand years ago, just as some from the *Kokinshu* might have been written yesterday. In putting together this anthology, we have been especially mindful, however, of including tanka that unmistakably belong to our own time and moment in history.

Consider, for example, this poem by Pamela Miller Ness about the death of her mother:

Autumn
of metastasis
she ticks
dozens of exotic lilies
in the bulb catalog.

Would it have been possible to write such a tanka in a Kyoto autumn one thousand years ago? Yes—a similar tanka probably was written. But no, this particular tanka could not have been written then.

Or consider this tanka, by John Barlow, about the loneliness of separation:

you talk on the phone
of wanting to watch it snow—
outside our window
the wind and rain
beat ceaselessly

This anthology offers a wide range of tones and topics, from William Ramsey, who out of his own daily trials writes wonderfully pithy, memorable tanka in a postmodern voice, to the monologues of Cherie Hunter Day, who documents her own variegated, interior landscapes as a naturalist does, finding in nature a correspondence between self and cosmos that can disturb us as much as reassure.

Nature is never far away; the imagery of tanka in English is in fact impossible without it. In these modern poems, the tanka poets revel in nature as they find it—

which may be in New York's Central Park as often as by a small stream in a mountain meadow. The following poem by Martin Lucas is about a nature peculiar to the twentieth century and an example of the kind of nature that tanka in English inhabit and compel us to witness:

> Dali paintings
> on the café wall
> the door wide open
> to a strange summer
> in a strange town

So also is this powerful evocation by ai li:

> on that night train
> to nowhere
> the leaves
> at
> my feet

What other kinds of tanka are found here? Look for poems of cultural alienation in Kenneth Tanemura, the lyrical in anne mckay and Christopher Herold, the wise and worldly in Francine Porad, Laura Maffei, Marianne Bluger, and Doris D. Kasson. In the vignettes, anecdotes, and diary-like notes of tanka by Jeff Witkin, Karina Young, Tom Clausen, and Fay Aoyagi, we find love, nature, and all the other subject matter of contemporary life.

Today's English-language tanka community exhibits the same characteristics found in other subcultures of the poetry world: a coterie of devoted readers and enthusiasts, scholars, translators, organizers, publishers of chapbooks and collections, editors, reviewers, competitions and awards, conferences, Web sites, Internet discussion groups and lists, journals and magazines, organizations, and celebrated, essential books. These features parallel similar "nesting" trends seen in other poetry subcultures, as well as in society generally, as people seek out and form semi-autonomous special-interest or support groups within an impersonal popular culture dominated by commodity- and celebrity-driven mass marketing and commercialism. Literary nesting becomes a means of both retrieving and building personal identity, establishing relationships with people who know you, pursuing goals and objectives that are held in common with others, and making room generally for one's own interests, tastes, and passions with fewer distractions. It is about making or finding meaning in a world that visits chaos and confusion upon the individual and at the same time withholds any true sense of personal worth, value, or relevance.

In recent years, the World Wide Web has become another means of publishing. On any given day, hundreds of new tanka by North American poets alone appear somewhere on the Web. This estimate is probably conservative, yet indicates an outpouring of

40,000 poems a year—a staggering sum.

The impact of the Internet has indeed been tremendous, permitting the formation of chat rooms and discussion groups that bring poets, editors, and enthusiasts across the globe into daily and weekly contact, sharing poems, discussing technique, formulating theories, and exchanging ideas.

In considering the niche tanka might occupy in English-language poetry, it is possible to make too much of its Japanese origins. Tanka written in English today shares many features with well-known, long-lived elements, forms, and styles of English verse, past and present. The irregularities and asymmetries of tanka seem especially compatible and comparable to those of contemporary free verse.

We might suspect that poetry of a few short lines would be capable of expressing only the simplest ideas or emotions, but that is not the case. Large ideas and complex emotions abound in tanka. Though their expression is highly compressed and the vocabulary outwardly direct, simple, and with little or no adornment, tanka have the power to handle large themes as well as evoke a single emotion. Tanka's frequent combination of natural imagery with personal introspection, reflection, or confession results in a kind of "subjective realism" that has a tonal register forceful enough that it could profoundly change the traditional short, reflective English lyric. A good tanka can clear the reader's mind while refilling it with something astonishing and unforgettable. Many such poems appear in this anthology.

Much of tanka's charm and power relates to its directness of expression, and this is one consequence of the form's brevity. The poem has little or no room for the use of contrivance, elaboration, complex argument, or other rhetorical treatment to convey an idea or evoke an emotion. When a tanka makes a political point, reveals some love interest, expresses a philosophy, comments on life, sends a message, eulogizes a dead person, gives advice, or complains about or mocks some aspect of life, it does so with energy and compression—it gets right to the point in a way that is new to the short poem in English. Similar to haiku, contemporary English-language tanka make poetic discoveries in the ordinary moments and scenes of daily life. Unlike haiku, tanka permit a range of speculation and transmutation to take place between the reality of things observed and the poet's distinct way of understanding, interpreting, and of lending or withholding meaning from the words he or she uses. The personality of the poet is present in most tanka, though frequently muted and very seldom the subject; in haiku, generally, the poet stands at a cognitive distance. Both tanka and haiku use implication, nuance, and suggestion in ways that are new to the short poem in English. The complexities that arise from ambiguity are inherent in both forms; however, tanka in English appear to share many more of the features and elements that typify most Western verse. Naturally, the poet's skill in orchestrating these elements is decisive: tanka provides no room to hide a fumble, conceal an unnecessary word, or mask a defect with padding or verbal costume.

The voice of each poet included in this anthology is distinct, individual. Each poet has made tanka an intimate, personal vehicle of poetic expression. Certain techniques and features, briefly discussed in the foregoing, are identifiable and held in common. These features define tanka as unique among the poetic forms and genres found in English literature. Its poets will undoubtedly use tanka to probe, push, and reshape the outer boundaries of the short-poem universe.

Tanka in English is still defining itself—chiefly through the poems. Hence, this book offers no conclusive formal definition of what tanka is, or what it aspires to be, beyond such descriptions, observations, and naming of parts as provided in the foregoing discussion. A definition of this sort is a little like trying to formulate the "theory of everything" that has kept physicists puzzled, frequently confused, and busy during most of the past seventy-five years. They still don't have that theory, but the universe goes on regardless.

The reader is warmly invited to discover what the tanka has to offer in its English-language flesh and bones. In these poems, we may learn to pay attention in a different way, and receive our news of the world with unexpected delight.

—*Michael McClintock*
Los Angeles, September 2003

Beichman, Janine. *Masaoka Shiki: His Life and Works*. Boston: Cheng & Tsui, 2002.

_____. *Embracing the Firebird: Yosano Akiko and the Birth of the Female Voice in Modern Japanese Poetry*. Honolulu, Hawaii: University of Hawai'i Press, 2002.

Carter, Stephen D., ed. and trans. *Traditional Japanese Poetry: An Anthology*. Stanford University Press, 1991.

_____, ed. and trans. *Waiting for the Wind: Thirty-six Poets of Japan's Late Medieval Age*. New York: Columbia University Press, 1989.

Cranston, Edwin, ed. and trans. *A Waka Anthology, Volume One: The Gem-Glistening Cup*. Stanford: Stanford University Press, 1993.

Goldstein, Sanford, and Seishi Shinoda, trans. *Red Light: Tanka by Mokichi Saito*. Lafayette, Indiana: Purdue University Press, 1989.

_____, and Seishi Shinoda, trans. *Romaji Diary and Sad Toys by Takuboku Ishikawa*. Boston: Tuttle Publishing, 2000.

_____, and Seishi Shinoda, trans. *Sad Toys, by Takuboku Ishikawa*. Lafayette, Indiana: Purdue University Press, 1977.

_____, and Seishi Shinoda, trans. *Tangled Hair: Selected Tanka from "Midaregam" by Akiko Yosano*. Boston: Cheng & Tsui Company, 2002 {a revised edition with a new preface based on the earlier editions of *Tangled Hair* published by Charles E. Tuttle, Rutland, Vermont, 1987, and Lafayette, Indiana: Purdue University Studies, 1971}.

Hamill, Sam, and Keiko Matsui Gibson, trans. *River of Stars: Selected Poems of Yosano Akiko*. Boston: Shambhala, 1997.

Hirshfield, Jane, and Mariko Aratani, trans. *The Ink Dark Moon: Love Poems by Ono noKomachi and Izumi Shikibu,*

Women of the Ancient Court of Japan. New York: Charles Scribner's Sons, 1986.

Huey, Robert N. *The Making of Shinkokinshu.* Manoa, Hawaii: University of Hawaii Press, 2002.

Keene, Donald, comp. and ed. *Anthology of Japanese Literature from the Earliest Era to the Mid-Nineteenth Century.* New York: Grove Press, 1955.

Lowitz, Leza, et al, eds. and trans. *A Long Rainy Season: Haiku & Tanka.* Berkeley, California: Stone Bridge Press, 1994.

Miner, Earl. *An Introduction to Japanese Court Poetry.* Stanford: Stanford University Press, 1968.

Reichhold, Jane, and Hatsue Kawamura, trans. *A String of Flowers, Untied . . . : Love Poems from the "Tale of Genji" by Murasaki Shikibu.* Berkeley, California: Stone Bridge Press, 2002.

Rexroth, Kenneth. *One Hundred Poems from the Japanese.* New York: New Directions, 1964.

Rodd, Laurel Rasplica, trans. *Kokinshu: A Collection of Poems Ancient and Modern* Boston: Cheng & Tsui Company, 1996.

Sato, Hiroaki, and Burton Watson, eds. and trans. *From the Country of Eight Islands: An Anthology of Japanese Poetry.* Seattle: University of Washington Press, 1981.

Sesar, Carl, trans. *Poems to Eat by Ishikawa Takuboku.* Tokyo: Kodansha International, 1966.

Smith, Susan Sutton, ed. *The Complete Poems and Collected Letters of Adelaide Crapsey.* Albany: SUNY Press, 1977.

Stamm, Jack, trans. *Salad Anniversary by Michi Tawara.* Tokyo: Kawade Shobo Shinsha, 1988.

Stevens, John, trans. *Lotus Moon: The Poetry of the Buddhist Nun Rengetsu.* New York: Weatherhill, 1994.

Ueda, Makoto. *Modern Japanese Tanka: An Anthology.* New York: Columbia University Press, 1996.

(For additional titles of collections and chapbooks by poets represented in this anthology, see the BIOGRAPHICAL NOTES section at the back of the book. Ce Rosenow's *Tanka in English: A Bibliography*, an exhaustive compilation of titles by these and other tanka poets, is available from the Tanka Society of America.)

Barlow, John. *Snow About to Fall*. Liverpool, England: Snapshot Press, 2003.

Chula, Margaret. *Always Filling, Always Full*. Buffalo, New York: White Pine Press, 2001.

Clausen, Tom. *Homework*. Liverpool, England: Snapshot Press, 2000.

Day, Cherie Hunter. *Early Indigo*. Liverpool, England: Snapshot Press, 2002.

Goldstein, Sanford. *This Tanka Whirl*. Coinjock, North Carolina: Clinging Vine Press, 2001.

Ogi, Saeko, and Amelia Fielden, trans. *Fountains Play & Time Passes: An Anthology of Tanka Poems in English and Japanese*. Charnwood, Australia: Ginninderra Press, 2002.

Reichhold, Jane, and Werner Reichhold, eds. *Wind Five Folded: An Anthology of English-Language Tanka*. Gualala, California: AHA Books, 1994.

Shelley, Pat. *Turning My Chair*. Foster City, California: Press Here, 1997.

St. Maur, Gerald, ed. *Countless Leaves*. Edmonton, Alberta: Inkling Press and Magpie Productions, 2001.

Tasker, Brian, ed. *In the Ship's Wake: An Anthology of Tanka*. North Shields, England: Iron Press, 2001.

Ward, Linda Jeannette, ed. *Full Moon Tide: The Best of Tanka*

Splendor 1990-1999. Coinjock, North Carolina: Clinging Vine Press, 2000.

Welch, Michael Dylan, ed. *Footsteps in the Fog.* Foster City, California: Press Here, 1994.

_____, ed. *Castles in the Sand: Tanka Society of America Members' Anthology.* Sammamish, Washington: Press Here, 2003.

MAGAZINES AND JOURNALS PUBLISHING TANKA IN ENGLISH

American Tanka, Laura Maffei, editor, P.O. Box 120-124, Staten Island, NY 10312.

Blithe Spirit: the Journal of the British Haiku Society, Colin Blundell, editor, Longhold, East Bank, Wingland, Sutton Bridge, Spalding, Lines PE12 9YS, UK.

Bottle Rockets. Stanford M. Forrester, editor, P.O. Box 290691, Wethersfield, CT 06129-0691.

Chrysanthemum, Koon Woon, editor, 202 6th Avenue, #1105, Seattle, WA 98104-2303.

Hummingbird: Magazine of the Short Poem. Phyllis Walsh, editor, P.O. Box 96, Richland Center, WI 53581.

Lilliput Review. Don Wentworth, editor, 282 Main Street, Pittsburgh, PA 15201.

Lynx. Jane Reichhold, editor, an Internet Web magazine at http://ahapoetry.com.

Mariposa. Claire Gallagher and Carolyn Hall, editors, 864 Elmira Drive, Sunnyvale, CA 94087.

New American Imagist. Michael McClintock, editor, Hermitage West, P.O. Box 124, South Pasadena, CA 91030-0124.

Paper Wasp. 7 Bellevue Terrace, St. Lucia, Queensland, 4067, Australia.

Presence. Martin Lucas, editor, 90 D Fishergate Hill, Preston PR1 8JD, UK.

RAW NerVZ Haiku. Dorothy Howard, editor, 67 Court Street, Aylmer, Quebec, Canada, J9H 4M1.

Tangled Hair. John Barlow, editor, Snapshot Press, P.O. Box 132, Crosby, Liverpool, L23 8XS, UK.

The Tanka Journal. Hatsue Kawamura, editor, *Nihon Kajin Club* (Japan Tanka Poets' Club), Shuei Building, 2F, 1-12-5, Higashi-Gotanda, Shinagawa-ku, Tokyo, 141-0022, Japan.

Tanka Light. Elizabeth St Jacques, editor, "Poetry in the Light" Internet Web site at <http://Startag.tripod.com/Contents.html>.

Tanka Society of America Newsletter. Pamela Miller Ness, ed., 33 RiversideDrive, Apt. 4-G, New York, NY 10023-8025.

Tundra: The Journal of the Short Poem. Michael Dylan Welch, ed., 22230 NE 28th Place, Sammamish, WA 98074-6408.

ORGANIZATIONS

Japan Tanka Poets' Club (*Nihon Kajin Club*), Shuei Bldg., 2F, 1-12-5, Higashi-gotanda, Shinagawa-ku, Tokyo, 141-0022, Japan.

Tanka Society of America, 22230 NE 28th Place, Sammamish, WA 98074-6408.

A brief word about how this anthology was compiled. The anthology editors, Michael McClintock, Pamela Miller Ness, and Jim Kacian were joined by four additional selectors: John Barlow, Sanford Goldstein, Laura Maffei, and Michael Dylan Welch. We first discussed and debated the goals and specific objectives such an anthology might have. Questions of scope, standards of selection, and dozens of important, peripheral issues were debated, argued, flayed, and racked. This consumed several months. Each selector then scoured hundreds of collections, magazines, and other sources for original tanka in English. Each selector was responsible for submitting an exhaustive list of all poets whose work he or she felt should be given initial consideration. All the lists were compared, compiled, and integrated into a master list of several hundred names. Because we wanted an anthology that would provide enough poems to enable the reader to form a sense of a poet's range, tone, and flavor, this list was obviously too long. We wanted an anthology that was deeper than publishing just one or two poems per poet. Amid much discussion, we sought to cut the list of nominated names by at last half. We often did additional research on particular poets, especially those unknown to certain selectors. Poems went back and forth and the work of poets was discussed in detail. We cut the list in half, and then cut it in half again. Each poet on our final list was invited to submit a large selection of both published and unpublished poems. The work of deceased poets was sought out through estate executors, relatives, or friends. Only in a few cases were we unable to locate a particular poet. Each selector had the opportunity (and used it) to persuade the others about the value of specific poems and the contributions of particular poets whom they especially liked. Cases for the inclusion of specific poems, or of particular poets, were won and lost by each selector. Always, our goal was to represent English-language tanka in its variety and accomplishments through its finest examples. We found a number of poems only after searching through numerous poetry books and journals, or poring through lengthy, unpublished material and other documents. Our selection of poets and our decisions to include or not include a particular poem were finally matters guided by intuition.

the
tanka
anthology

ai li

a quiet night
a quiet moon
teeth
dropping into
glass

river rain
re-telling
your daughter
your stories
in my voice

on that night train
to nowhere
the leaves
at
my feet

i find a lake
to drown my past in
leave my shoes behind
for you
to forget

late at night
no one in
i ring
my
own doorbell

at twilight
a lone cyclist
on a back road
finds me
lonelier

christmas eve
i'm up all night
hanging
my face
in baubles

reading you
that fable
at bedtime
my wings
in shadow

the last train
in a dream
i get on it
with
the embalmer

moonlight
in the yard
and on
the rooftiles
I cannot sleep

through rain
through a year
of threadbare melodies
the early dark
of stolen mulberries

Kay F. Anderson

Gone wandering
in a rice paper brush painting,
trees and grasses sway
and the red kite takes flight
in my heart

You say this
small dish of red ink will last
my whole life . . .
I hesitate now to
use my signature stamp.

a marsh hawk
up from the feeder
flies off with a finch
  such a small cry
  wrapped in talons

Fay Aoyagi

Indian summer—
I jaywalk
to avoid a man
I slept with
once

a farmer's market
I pick up an eggplant
small enough to
fit in my palm
. . . Pearl Harbor anniversary

8

a tofu shop is gone
the school is renovated . . .
the same
mugs and plates
in my parents' cupboard

spring equinox
convinced by
magnolia blossoms
I bought a multi-colored
shower curtain

my father
rolled
his first cigarette
with a page torn
from an English dictionary

cherry blossom storm
in the shrine
for war gods . . .
weight of the history
on my umbrella

the names etched
on Vietnam Memorial Wall—
rice noodles for the one
who fought
not to go

a first kiss—
I wonder
if I should tell him
about my missing
uterus

passing a maternity dress shop
my flat belly reflected
on the window
I am not jealous of
mannequins

with a man
who was once
the center of my universe
I discuss
interest rates

passing the artichoke fields
dotted with migrant workers—
have you thought why
I feel closer
to them

Pamela Babusci

i am
a prisoner
in this
snowflake
melt me

scattered lovers
never a husband
these cherry trees
raining petals
everywhere, nowhere

fastening
an antique barrette
into my newly washed hair
i miss his hands that used
to center perfectly

i remove my cross
before we lie down . . .
together we make
shadows
on the wall

not a single star
out of place in the
milky way—
the garden gate
left ajar all night

John Barlow

dawn
and you open
your deep-green eyes—
blackbirds stir
somewhere in the conifers

summer
and the pair of us
barefoot
on the melting
country lanes

the way you are sleeping,
the smile on your lips—
if this were my darkest hour
I would have no need
to wake you now

away from home . . .
long strands
of your hair
tangled
with my belongings

sitting alone
in the seaside café
my apple pie
arrives with an extra squirt
of imitation cream

hours
before daybreak—
the gap
between us
our bodies cannot warm

you talk on the phone
of wanting to watch it snow—
outside our window
the wind and rain
beat ceaselessly

just five minutes
pressed against a stranger
on a crowded train
so why do I spend my day
dreaming of a life with her?

snow
about to fall . . .
both of us know
we have both
been waiting

in the dark
a tawny owl calls
unanswered
I pour out my last drip
of whisky

a quiet moment
to myself . . .
my shadow plays
slow shadow bass
on the back wall

together at last
watching these slim diving grebes
pair for the first time
I wonder whether you sense
I'm feeling kind of past it

unexpectedly
an indian summer
but now you've gone
just who am I supposed
to waste it with

something missing,
this warm autumn morning
a feeling
I've carried with me
all these years

Marianne Bluger

In the cold shade
of office towers
a bus-stop stranger
with the eyes
of a man who knows

Chewing an oyster
in a fogbound inn
too late
I feel my teeth
grind pearl to grit

On the night train
through that foreign land
I waver once
glimpsing
a lit farm kitchen

Just visiting
my friend in the asylum
I too start to see
each happy face
as a fascist device

on Cape Cod
in a midnight supermarket
I spot the Virgin
a teen—serenely pregnant
pushing a mop pail with her foot

turning
from my daughter's anger
to watch
grey dishwater
swirl down the drain

Almost invisible
the zero
I traced
just last week
in the mantle dust . . .

on our way
to the coast—a wasp
flies in
and down the road a bit
out again

real
as a dream
the little beetle
shimmers—green
on my upturned palm

through midnight rain
with the radio on
by the dash light
I study the man
with whom I am crossing the continent

Night falls
& the Nam vet
with his camera
prowls the campground
snapping rabbits

Janice M. Bostok

the sky becomes
an extension of
the lake . . .
what is there
but another day

beginning
a journey:
winter wind
taking the door from my hands
as it opens

awake
the long night caressing you
in dawn light
a young cock crows
still not getting it right

in half sleep
an involuntary orgasm
more gentle
as you have been
since your stroke

Naomi Y. Brown

red mushroom
I know that
it's poison
but my heart desires
to touch it

no one
visits me
long autumn night
listening to
"Fantasia"

when
you are gone
I will buy a robot
as my companion
cherry blossoms

Marjorie Buettner

this morning
the cold of your absence
a presence now
shall I dress it like scarecrows
standing in an empty field

vacation's end
the highway still unraveling
when I close my eyes
how many parts of myself
have I left homeless behind

late summer
wild roses have taken over
the garden path
how their scent beckons me
wanting more than I dare

spring rain
scent of these ink black streets
washed clean
is there time enough ever
to start over again

thunderstorms
threading their way
through the city
this uncontrollable desire
to run naked in the rain

Margaret Chula

after the cease fire
refugees from Chechnya
return to rubble
   sparrows weave the hair of children
   into their spring nests

my friends tell me
that they are breaking up
I stand at the sink
—rinse the cloudy rice over
and over again

the black negligee
that I bought for your return
hangs in my closet
  day by day plums ripen
  and are picked clean by birds

how old are you now
my father asks me
and when I tell him
his shoulders sag
into the present

you sign your letters
'affectionately'
I write, 'loving you'
picking a scab on my cleavage
I watch it bleed

Tom Clausen

every few bounces
the robin pauses on the lawn
to look and listen;
as if that were all
there was to do

she's not here
to see it
but after breaking the stick
I perfectly fit the broken ends
back together again

I had it all
figured out,
this little wisdom of mine
then in the night
the rain so hard

the house quiet
and cold
this early morning alone—
saddened to know how much
I desired just this

as I sit in thought
she moves briskly
around the room
stirring the chill
in the air

it's not for
any simple reason
I've fallen out
of love
with my life

between chores
I study my hands
as if they might hold
something
I should know

it occurs to me
to retreat
from this world,
as if another world
might exist

quite by surprise
my daughter asks me
if I'd like to be a woman
  the gravity in the moment
  I took to answer

my beer gone flat
but out of duty
I finish it—
living all these
middle aged days

  as useless
  as this hard rain
  on frozen ground—
  these memories of all the people
  I once was . . .

Gerard John Conforti

On this autumn day
sitting alone on the steps
outside the dark house
only the sound of the leaves
falling against the brick walls

Now and then
the clouds cover the morning sun
and it pours rain
but, today, the sky is clear and blue
and I turn to face the winds

every day that passes
like the wind in grass
brings memories
of long ago
in a field of dreams

Geoffrey Daniel

I built that wall
set my initials in concrete
deep, with the trowel.

What more can a man do
before the moss comes, and the frost?

it is a pale horse
ambling to meet us across
the darkening field;

flaunting bruises on their arms,
boy soldiers in Vukovar

was there ever
on this one's pearls
the taste of salt
the cracked hands
of the fisherman?

ebbtide—the dinghies
turn on their leashes, tugging
for the horizon;

waves dumping their burdens here,
at the loose edge of silence

Cherie Hunter Day

watching
the pear tree blossom
a new sorrow—
this year it is my turn
to leave

a long lunch—
pushing crumbs together
on the tablecloth
already this silence
between us

the music box
strains of *Au Claire de la Lune*—
as a child
wanting to free the dancer
beneath the glass dome

flash of white
during the quick flight
of a mockingbird
even though I am awake
something of the dream world

waiting past midnight
for an unobstructed moon
with its milky light
I can see clearly
the recesses of my heart

you asked
for an account of my day—
the amaryllis bud
is a crimson fist
sheathed in pale, pale green

through patterned glass
see how the water bends
the flower stems
my heart and many other
optical illusions

far more often
than in previous years
we argue—
I stack blue mussel shells
one inside the other

news of his death
I can only stare
at my hands
soil beneath my fingernails
with faint white moons

clear night, owl night
through the tissue of darkness
an exchange
their grip of honed surfaces
my sinew and bone

returning
to this shore year after year
all the broken shells
where we scattered
her ashes

Melissa Dixon

shimmering shapes
above the dark hills
northern lights
imagining I feel
magnetic fingers

low slow breathing
lying on our backs melting
in late-summer heat
the scent of fading lilies
hovers above the lawn

the secluded park
that someone used to tend
now you are gone
wild grasses hide the log
where once we held each other

Patricia Donegan

will I know the last moment
as I did this morning over breakfast
noticing the sunlight on my bare hand
no rings, bracelet or watch
naked as a bone

I long to be a lone pine tree
on top of a rocky mountain
where only old women come
in the pale light of the moon
to burn candles in the darkness

Tonight
like many without a lover
I'm going to bake bread
push my knuckles
into soft dough

Jeanne Emrich

dry seeds scatter
from my hand into the wind—
one clings
as if to say there is in me
something yet to be

old pine,
every spring you drop
another perfect branch
and all I do is just
lay down my pen

today my heart
is a white magnolia
in early spring
I do not hesitate
to risk everything

not thinking really
I just roll paint
over five years of your life
and admire how it
freshens up the room

don't take me
into your old age
with you, mother—
even the waning moon
keeps its distance

Amelia Fielden

I wanted
to say how much I
admire you, but
we parted there, still
talking of plum jam

halving fruit,
my second husband's
way of love—
hard to change habits
so late in life

my father
died again last night—
in other dreams
grandmother still lives
until the day breaks

Stanford M. Forrester

autumn clouds
pass my window
one by one—
i fill the vase on the table
with bittersweet

i keep your memory
stored away
somewhere
how else could i have
such sad, sad thoughts

sitting, watching
the sand
in the Zen garden
blow away . . .
this autumn wind

Coney Island boardwalk—
kissing you
in the photobooth
when everything
was black & white

Garry Gay

Age spots
now stain your photograph
taken so long ago
I wonder how kind
time has been to you

You rise to leave
saying you have a busy day
planned for tomorrow
but what about this moment
I planned for all week

A quick hug
then off we go
each in a new direction
we are both too busy
for this moment of sorrow

I place
in the time capsule
memories of you
who now will discover
your mysterious ways?

She was my lover
now I watch her
talk to him
I have become only bones
in the desert

Sanford Goldstein

snow
piling
a crane's wing
wings across
this bare mind

tonight's
Van Gogh
shoes
damp through
by the kitchen door

I am a lump
of thought
this fragmented night
of insect cry
and crawl

no red wheelbarrow
to make
all the difference—
no, but these pines!
these cranes!

Buddha,
pour me a cup of poetry
from your warm mouth
this empty
night

Anne Frank,
how your scribbled,
endured,
and now I tramp up these stairs
they hurried you down

       at times, mother,
       with your peripheral vision
       you called me by some other name
       as if you wanted
       twice the love

swept up
into my own
Saturday night fever,
I settle for less,
I tanka my way out

only a one-sentence
rebuke
to my kid
and all day
the lousy after-taste

frying
breaded cauliflower
on my two-burner
I watch the browniing,
I turn, I control

lull me, muse,
into the wavering belief
that my tanka
will walk me
to the end of the road

LeRoy Gorman

my father dead
good for him
he waited
until I too
had white hair

sometimes
is all it says
a torn page
wind brings
with blossoms

in the glovebox
when the car is sold
a map from our honeymoon
still open to a place
we never got

with this ax I remember
my father trimmed trees
for my mother
to see the river
she remembered

the phone rings twice
& no one is there
& the phone rings
again & again
& again

with the latest news
off come
the estrogen patches
off come
the storm windows

at the funeral of
one who said
God is dead
God is
dead

old
pines point
to a warmer place
the years
we've been together

not a word
about the suicidal friend
until the mail is returned
MOVED / UNKNOWN //
DEMENAGE / INCONNU

Caroline Gourlay

the same room
the same view
the same year—
and the way this music
could make me believe it

watching you
as you kneel to lay the fire,
your back bent
your hair quite grey now
I decide against it

after
your death
your halfworked tapestry—
picking it out of the
wastepaper basket

you climb
a speck on the rockface
of the mountain—
waiting here below it is
I who am exposed

sitting beside you
I avoid your eyes but
reach out my hand
as if offering you something
you might need one day

Yvonne Hardenbrook

as you sit
for my portrait of you
I tingle and burn—
everything I have longed for
at the very tip of my brush

the blizzard
I thought I was prepared for
fills the patio
between me and the shed
where the snow shovel is

down on my knees
with a new cat's-eye shooter
fresh out of the bag—
debating whether to send
the marbles to my grandson

facelift
and orthodontia
    I strain
  to recognize
    my sister

you ask
what I want most
this   I say
as we nightwalk
the hills of home

Christopher Herold

mist swirls
beneath a sea-cliff pine
I stop to rest
my hand on the weathered trunk
bent by years of compromise

high tide
not quite reaching this rock
spring moon
I know it wasn't your intention
to make me yearn

in her convertible
she talks about power
and guns the engine . . .
leaning back, I gaze up
at the redwoods

when the poppies close
I'll turn my back on the wind
and walk home
through tall meadow grasses
wishing not even for you

rain at last . . .
in a torrent of words
my child's confession
of innocence lost
we walk until the ground is soft

small umbrella—
from the tips of its spokes
cold rain falls
onto her left shoulder
into my right coat pocket

butterflies
in this hedge-encircled garden
she leans on my arm
and, listening to me read,
falls in love with my father

in morning fog
we ship the oars and drift
between loon calls
all that's left of this world
the warmth of our bodies

in a graveyard
wandering with the shadows
of spring clouds . . .
how do I decide which grasses
to have removed for her?

autumn dusk
the sound of her loom shuttle
weaving memories
spun from the hair
of our old dog

Jean Jorgensen

your name and address
and phone . . . crossed out everywhere
still I can't believe
it is really you under
this dark frozen mound

swallowing tears
as heavy footsteps approach
my husband's hands
so large around mine
here on the psych ward

he's traveled
these highways most of his life
yet today
somewhere between anger and tears
old man admits he is lost

Jim Kacian

fresh cement
attracts the hand
like amber
each fingerprint
reveals me

a purple azalea
has bloomed
to February
we have done well
to find this place

i will not write
a poem of silence
and moonlight
i will just
let them be

kirsty karkow

strong wind—
flowers and leaves turn
inside out
a door slams, and I welcome
my mother for a visit

torrid day
broken by thunder
quick and sharp
this streak of anger
sadly misdirected

december sunrise
even the usual crows
absolutely still
this brief moment between
the in-breath and the out-breath

Doris Kasson

whenever i notice
i give it a nudge
our wedding picture
hanging there still
ever so slightly askew

afterwards
clearing out his desk
I find him
in bits and pieces
the man I never knew

they seem
to pile up on my side
of the bench
kids and
falling leaves

sundays she talks
of sin and salvation
while I go fishing
in my old tackle box
to find the perfect lure

he uses them
over and over
disposable things
I was so sure
he'd hang onto me

nestled together
he speaks of romance
i of the merits
of simple declarative
sentences

invited at last
to meet his parents
i find myself
wondering which me
i should wear

learning
a new language in this
my old age
i start with the word
for goodbye

calling her
by his first wife's name
how quickly
they come
clouds in a summer sky

heart pounding
i pray not now
lord
poem unfinished
hair a mess

not too unpleasant
the growling sound
of the shredder
cutting up
the story of my life

Michael Ketchek

in the language
of the old country
that I can't read
letters my father kept
from his long dead friend

her husband
suddenly appears
in the conversation—
pouring milk into coffee
I notice it's gone bad

not having it all
is hard—her friends
and the women's magazines
all say
it's his fault

carefully
selecting the asparagus
as if it mattered
she is
gone

the limp wind sock
reminds him
of the side effects
of taking prozac
but who cares

Larry Kimmel

looking down
on that distant page
of meadow—

a railroad train straight as a sentence
and I too mountain high to read its noise

around the campfire
singing with the others,
I flick an unworthy thought
from my mind—
a spark from my sleeve

as twilight gathers,
the white boulder in
the stone fence
grows luminous—
some things take a lifetime

for fifty years
through all the weathers
of the mind,
I have loved the world with my eye
. . . if nothing else—that

when I think
that we may never
meet again . . .
this hillside of aspens
endlessly fluttering

still angry,
I hear an acorn
bouncing down
the branches of the oak—
my fist flowers to catch it

I'm just saying
how good it is to see her
when suddenly
she sticks out her tongue—
catches a snowflake

touch . . . touch . . .
the skipping stone hits
the farther bank . . .
suddenly I am old
and understand nothing

walking
the railroad tracks
alone—
more and more we live
our parallel lives

Robert Kusch

Tossing a stone
into the dark well, I am
suddenly five years old
—waiting to hear from
the other side of the world

Lightning on
the horizon
my child
takes a huge
bite from a pear

For a moment
at the field's full length—
mid-morning shadows
creeping back to
their trees

Past midnight,
walking out beyond the town
where I grew up

. . . . cottonwoods brushing
the winter moon

It wants us
to go
no further—
this roadside
yarrowscent

Leatrice Lifshitz

writing
on the back of the letter
she wrote to me
    a poem about windows
    and distance

a gravel road
following the river's curve—
the breast I don't have
    bouncing along with the one
    that's real

all her things
put into bags and boxes—
face down
    on the elevator floor
    a tiny photograph

I
    who am not really
    a cook
poke gently into
    a green pepper

Geraldine Clinton Little

on a marigold,
orange, edged with crimson, the white
    butterfly, wings touched
with crimson—I long to paint
    the similar differences

ah summer, summer,
how quickly you fade. I cut
      rusted zinnias,
place them on a glassed table-
      top, as if time could double

bringing in cattails
I bring in, too, remembrance
      of the geese veeing
above them in frosted air—
      all this in my plain stone jar

so democratic
you are, moon, lighting the whore's
      way home and the priest's,
the cricket's too and the owl's
      as daybreak blurs your brightness

by moonlight we set
small candles afloat—no use
        to Hiroshima's
dead, just to us believing
        light enlightens a dark world

I sit in full sun
naked beside my hut house.
        a butterfly finds
my left breast—I meditate
        a long time on our meshed lives

the Concorde crosses
ancient sea lanes as I watch
     it spin to a speck.
more wonderful, surely to
     drift under sail to Cathay

eating a lobster
I stop to think of the deep
     sea lanes it traveled
before this death. I won't, friend,
     leave even shells when *I* go

Martin Lucas

on Ascension Day
looking to the sky
swifts
spin on the wind
rain falls

awake past midnight
I feel the odd vertigo
of being alone
the balcony light flickers
high above: a few faint stars

futile task
shuffling information
I face a screen
with the news of your dying
and nowhere to file it

hordes of sightseers
no one seems to see
the red-tailed hawk
spiralling the air
above Niagara

stuck for conversation
at the seafood restaurant
in every soup spoon
a spinning
ceiling fan

my wife's lover
walks straight past me
wearing my wife's hat
I remember the fit of it
on my own head

we talk of poetry
and the politics of poetry
on barbed wire
an unexploded
orange balloon

Dali paintings
on the café wall
the door wide open
to a strange summer
in a strange town

damselflies
mate
at the carp pond
we walk the same path
apart

the rattle of hangers
in an empty wardrobe
this cold room
that used to be yours
and now is mine

the many night noises of London
subside
in the smallest hour
all that's left:
voice of the blackbird

Laura Maffei

Halloween—
infant Batman
in my arms
barely aware of this world
that needs saving

energy waning
as the afternoon wears on
a grim co-worker
leans into my cubicle
whispering conspiracy

the clock on the wall
looks the same as yesterday
at fifteen past three,
but in my pocket mirror
I check my face for lines

tucked away
inside the gray metal drawer
of the desk
of a middle manager:
a book about angels

in this crazy March
the winds blow hot and cold
with indecision
and my house is a tempest
of disordered underwear

amid the jumping
of this afternoon dance class
I hold in my gaze
the sweaty image
of my twenty-eighth year

ovulating
this rainy evening
after work
I grin widely
at every man on the bus

from the confines
of this beige cubicle
I send e-mail
stating my intention
to run away to Greece

morning—
taking a phone call
from a recruiter
my bathrobe
falls open

as if she feels
how much I am missing you
already
a girl near me on the plane
begins to weep

in the dark
like an old wise woman
I give advice
to five American girls
from my narrow hostel cot

Thelma Mariano

I am alone
with the sound of rapids
constantly churning
tonight this river
will not sleep

years on my own
I still stare after
a white-haired couple
the way his body
shields her from the wind

rows of petunias
all pink and evenly spaced
to think
my life could have been
that predictable

the morning after—
rinsing plates in the sink
I watch suds
slide off the porcelain
and remember your hands

Michael McClintock

biting
into the peach
it seemed
it did
kiss me

raindrops
fall among
the flowers
ants explore
my face

carrying the sun, the clouds,
the mountains easily—
   a small stream
   wandering unnamed
   in this wild place

a bird out on the prairie
bathing at a pool
the starlight
thrown down
the singing throat

   next door
   the lovemaking
   subsides
   stars fall
   from other worlds

folding
her death robe—
the less bright
reverse-side
of the fabric

an old photo
of my parents
young and happy—
    of all the things I own
    that is the saddest

Yale-educated
impeccably dressed
how reasonably
the probate attorney explains
fucking the dead

the moon tonight
a humid bean
I imagine men and women
climbing down from it
on thin, silver ladders

the poets tell us
love is painful—
is that what you think?
if I love you, will you suffer
so very much?

here's a guy
sits on his mat
like Buddha
but here's one
that just sits

anne mckay

shopkeepers
of earlymorning
unwind the night awning
        a dazzle
        of white apron

scent of blue flowers
        still
in the hot nightstudio
        opening my door to a small sleep
        a cooler blue

woman
        leaning
from a latenightwindow
                        closing the shutters
                        closing the moon

centered
        by north light
the potter's wheel
                small dreams
                curve within her hands

sometimes the wraith of a wild girl
                        a green girl
shimmers still
                in the clearing
                in the morning

Lenard D. Moore

glowing moon
shadow comes and goes
through the doorway
she raises her legs
around my neck

moon over the cottage
even the curves
of her body
filled with light,
the beads of sweat

deep summer
the smell of nail polish
on the bus
and the swift speaking
of two Spanish women

Funeral Parlor
a black man rolls the casket
down the crowded aisle,
little by little his shoes
shadow/shine in the white light

grandma frying
black skillet full of catfish
this wet afternoon
big brown boy sucking fishbones
and leaning over the sink

Matt Morden

when I have died
scatter my ashes across
the river island
between the two salmon pools
where driftwood wraps around alders

frost hollows
on the Somme battlefield
where granddad was shot
carrying whisky
for the officers

away from home
on business
I find the plate
from her doll's house
in my small change

covers pulled back
in the redness of dawn
i lie by myself
and watch my mind clear
to the chatter of birds

the brightest green
of weeping willow
leaves the call of church bells
up the valley
all in vain

June Moreau

What's on the other side
of the sky, Coyote?
Open the white door
of silence
and take me there . . .

For my long journey
through the Universe
a coat
is fashioned for me
from a remnant of sky

sun-smoke rises
from the pond
and white cranes
on the paper fan
lift their wings

scattering them
along the trail
to the summit
the poems I wrote
on pieces of birch bark

When the cello
is reluctant
use me
for your bow—
I am the autumn wind

such a fine feeling
this morning
even the air
is paper enough
for a poem

a green bowl
filled with them
beside my bed—
the apple-fragrance
of my sleep

it is woven
into the tapestry
of the meadow
with blue threads of rain—
the wild iris

Rice pudding—
how good it tastes
after the rain
with cherry petals
sticking to my window.

Pamela Miller Ness

Dear May Sarton,
bequeath me your phoenix
soaring rom granite slab
and whispering words
to this wet green world.

Today
my fifty-first birthday,
a sleeve
of this new silk blouse
tinged with lily pollen.

After
the diagnosis:
the taste
of bite after bite of this
buttered bread.

Autumn
of metastasis
she ticks
dozens of exotic lilies
in the bulb catalog.

Collecting
your clothes from the Home
I uncover
my unopened envelope.
Autumn's end.

Mother
under a morphine moon—
the man
in the cherrypicker
trims dead trees.

Apart
only hours:
a rainbow
at Narada Falls
cuts this chill mist.

November chill—
tangles of silver caught
in my brush.
Tell me
I'm still yours.

Soft rain
after a downpour.
Beneath
the worn coverlet
we sleep touching toes.

Like Chagall's
floating lovers
hold me
tethered only
to air.

Night
of the summit ascent
the sky full of stars.
No longer needing
to ask why.

Francine Porad

some cathedrals
take a century to build;
a fanatic
straps a bomb to himself . . .
the flight of birds

morning sun
seeps into
these weak bones;
I close my eyes
to escape the too-red geraniums

Michaelangelo
tapped his Moses on the knee
arise and walk!
I kiss the cherry-red mouth
on the canvas

photos fall
from the envelope;
he writes
he loved me then
before he knew men

I paint
the flamboyant butterfly,
its red markings . . .
all the while desiring you
rosy with heat

a woman
holds the waving child high
as the train passes
where . . . when . . .
did summer disappear

inscrutable face
at the hospital window . . .
a flock of starlings
swerve and dip
with the winter wind

Mama
on her hospital bed:
beyond vogue
without lipstick
without rouge

holding
her hand,
I reach
inside
the coma

van with my mother
rounds the corner—
that red body bag . . .
who would ever dream
red

I drop
a sprig of orchids
onto the casket,
thud
loud as never

Carol Purington

That dream again
floating weightless like a ghost
or astronaut
   the attic where my small bare toes
   stepped over dead wasps

Weeks isolated
   from those without the virus
My baby brother
   learning to take steps
My body learning not to walk

Her sharp knife quick
to peel, core, slice the red apple
    we talk of childhood fears
        how I blocked my ears
        against the fairy tale

First picking
a yellow rose then a pink one
    because I don't know
        how to be satisfied
        with one kind of beauty

He returns at dusk,
wild strawberries cupped pink
in his hard palm
    I eat their sweetness one by one
    and we talk about the day

A dream blows away
in a blaze of copper leaves
     my fingers grow cold
          as I gather color
          for a vase of winter-blue

Smell of narcissus
heavy as death in the room
     where the great-grandmother
forgets the faces
of those she birthed

The river runs away
yet never leaves its source
     always with me
          the tang of days when I walked
          another path

Indigo bird
who climbed the continent
to perch in white lilacs
    I too am weary
    of this pilgrim way

The white bear that walks
the borders of my world
in narrowing circles—
    one rosy dawn I will see death's tracks
    pool with pink light

That tipped-over maple tree—
its deep roots released from earth
by too much rain
    I also want to end my days .
    where I have always lived

William Ramsey

wanting so much
to dig up
the bones
of my dead son
and wash them

removing my arm
to paddle the boat
  advancing
  in the direction
  of my reach

this night
i will clasp with love
your silent waist
my dear and
tragic pen

a gnat's smudge
on my forearm—
the smallest death
i have known this year
but typical

three girls
coming down the sidewalk—
one with new breasts
seeking my eyes
for just a moment

When i am gone
you can search the sands
to find my name.
Do it quickly,
say the crabs.

one day
i'll throw my stomach
over the shoulder
and beg my way
to paradise

floating there
in the pickle jar
my writing hand
will survive me,
and maybe write of joy

this road
connecting to another
that to another
until reaching the spot
where i will turn cold

the hole
in my abdomen
is where
i've let her criticisms
pass through

where is it now,
my severed appendix—
in a bag,
with gall bladder, spleens,
and toes of strangers

Jane Reichhold

night
cry of a bird
without color
tear of a woman
dark

hot strawberry
tongue of a boy
ripe in early June
just out of school
bent over in a field

a broken tooth
yet he sees the young girl
naked before him
smiling a wide smile
as she was at twenty

a dead brown seed
becoming in a muddy pot
a white flower
it is a lie you know
about death I mean

a token of our love
broken as you take
the moon
the bright half you leave me
as something to cling to

soundless
octave of a piano
west windows
pillar of sun
play on the rug

in the pantry
canned tomatoes explode
the mess remains
charged with my guilt
for something I did not do

hair clean and long
sun-dried in the wind
my face
searches the blue sky
for its final destination

pink—a tanka sequence

dusk ripples
as we move from mauve
shadows step
out of the way before
the sureness coming together

knotted
his biceps pressed me against
the lace of his gown
low-cut and revealing
a few dark chest hairs

pointed
the toes of our high heels
slid together
in the space between my legs
a swelling in two sizes

musk
sweetened sweat slipped
between us
shapes rose and blue
in the hot jazz riffs

dizzy without breath
time rolled into one
past life
we have been together before
now male; now female

David Rice

mountain meadow
one tiger lily
sways above the lupine
I wanted to stand out too
but all I show is years

spring cleaning—
look at all this junk
we still have
the broken plastic plate
our son once painted

after the storm
a dead hummingbird
on our porch
I didn't want to pick it up
then didn't want to put it down

you nap
after our weekend away
hand on my thigh
I drive with one hand
on yours

Edward J. Rielly

black hole
somewhere out there
pulling in
what cannot be held
against the darkness

beyond the stadium
foul ball floating
out of sight—
my friend and I discuss
windshields and childhood

my birdfeeder
sways in the wind
with a swallow
holding steadfastly
to something certain

traveling the path
through rustling cornfields
to the cow pasture
I see father waving his cap
just before I wake up

first leaves fall
while you gently place
a sheet over
the flower bed, holding,
a bit longer, our summer

Alexis Rotella

Pear blossoms
fall in the moonlight;
in the silence
I embroider a quilt
for my single bed.

Holding a letter
with words no longer true;
day-lilies open
and wither
in the same vase.

After the rain
the peonies lie in heaps;
we talk about old lovers
and the men
who never loved us back.

(for Adele)

A swallowtail settles
on a cushion of coxcomb;
higher and higher we swing
into the flowers
of the sorrel.

New Year's Eve—
on a ladder
a moon-faced man
washes the face
of a clock.

Philip Rowland

pre-dawn blackness.
the wind has turned the sea
against itself . . .
we've grown into each other
and on into what's left

weight
of the rainy season—
knowing less
and less, and trusting
this is progress

stars
but no moon . . .
following
steps down
to the crematorium

Afraid—that
neither of us
can give . . .
what neither
of us needs

autumn rain
comes into its own
at dusk
becoming
one with my lust

Pat Shelley

Not to disturb
the spider in her web
between two trees
I take
the other path

I tell my guardian angel
I'll happily die
in April
alas, each April comes
and I tell her I'm not ready

At the opera
listening to a tenor
I never really liked—
when she put out her hand
and he took it, all was changed

My perfect son
cross with me
on Mother's Day
because I am not also
perfect

When your mother died
—my grandmother
I saw you weeping
under a veiled hat
holding your own hand

Sometimes
if I just turn my chair
around
the forms of things are not
as they were a moment ago

Soiled and creased
in the shape of his hand
his garden glove
left on the workbench
in the potting shed

The year after your death
all the pelargoniums you loved
froze one winter night
ten winters later
I am not yet consoled

It was a long time ago
we pricked our fingers
wrote our names in blood
on each other's wrists
—a long time ago

You who made us all
must I learn everything
in one brief life?
Couldn't you arrange that I come back
and learn part of it later?

I leave these poems
testament
that I was here
also these white roses
azaleas and chrysanthemum

Ruby Spriggs

a sudden loud noise—
all the pigeons of Venice
at once fill the sky
that's how it felt when your hand
accidentally touched mine

always too busy
to notice sunrise, sunset
even the full moon
now there is six feet of earth
covering your lovely eyes

a neighbour's door slams
a lover's quarrel perhaps
is this envy
trying to pick
an argument with you

day creeps up
from the horizon
clouded in mist
by sunset perhaps
there will be answers

25 floors up
I live in a lovely sky
below me
earthlings trudging
through a cold white world

After Chemo—a tanka sequence

I brush my hair—
by the handful
it comes out
so this is the day
my hair is set free

up my nose
and in my mouth
a hair covered pillow
again today
I wear a hair shirt

like the spider's threads
the sun catches
every one
of my hairs
on the floor

my friend
with curly hair says
"it may grow back curly"
I was content
with my straight hair

what a pack-rat I was
when was it I began
sorting through
discarding the toys
of this life

Elizabeth St Jacques

between snow spots
a butterfly brown and white
on pine needles—
to know brightness and calm
in this cold world

in full bright light
the graceful rise and fall
of the bluebird's wings
　　you came to me
　　so long ago like this

winding trail . . .
even the lowly snail
leaves a little silver
　　i turn to analyze
　　my thin path

Gerald St. Maur

On grey crushed rock,
an orange butterfly settling
between iron rails
creeping from infinity
with their ever coming train

Just out of earshot,
the periodic blinking
of a night airplane,
not quite far enough away
to be as close as the stars

Where has she gone to,
she who dialed the wrong number?
her apology
from the ether of angels
coming along copper wire

On the left-hand page
her attack in court met his
on the right-hand page;
but only when the book closed
did their words touch each other

Art Stein

my fingers
above the keyboard
waiting—
my indulgent muse
late, as usual

from the pond
quick, golden flashes
as the koi
change directions . . .
talk of her leaving

Each foot
in a different river,
rush
of wild colors
in each eddy.

the sun and
moon in the same sky,
sea of small
green leaves—opening day
at the farmer's market.

news
of the death of
a friend's child
reddens the scar
of an old wound

through the fog
of our last evening
your taillights
pulsing on and off
down the rutted drive

releasing
your warm body from
my mind,
your recent letter propped
against my cold juice glass.

barefoot
on warm sand
my toes
inches from the whole
Atlantic Ocean

returning at dusk
to watch the sea swallow
the west sun,
sunburn pushing through
my damp cotton shirt

John Stevenson

June
and the leaves
so green
I almost
tell the truth

parting with
my telescope
and with it
a certain way
of seeing myself

so clear, years later
that when he called his daughter
a "heartbreaker"
it was not my heart
he had in mind

I had read
your love poems
and now,
having met you,
read them again

A subway train,
traveling beside ours,
veers up and away.
My feelings for you
go where they go.

the leaves
were just budding
when you left
later you claimed
I could have stopped you

the ring itself
I don't remember
as much as
the mark it left
when it came off

However young I was
when I stopped wanting
to stay up all night,
I knew it as a step toward death
and felt it as a relief

of course
the summer sky
is beautiful
I mustn't hate them
for saying it so often

Still a newcomer
to this rural village.
For how many years
have our hedges grown a little more
than we have trimmed them?

autumn street . . .
some leaves pause
in blowing by
one day, I just thought
enough grieving

George Swede

I re-read
my brother's
suicide note—
tomatoes ripen
on the sill

Last night I felt
the first autumn chill
or was this my way
of understanding
what you said to me

Side-by-side
the way they used to sit
on the country store porch
the three old timers
in their graves

Writing a poem
of longing for her
I'm irritated
by the interruption
of her phone call

Cold winter morning—
as I wait for the call
a white hair falls
from my head
and sticks to the phone

Up at the first
crack of dawn
and planning
my naps
for the day

Crowded bar
the jackhammer operator
parodies his job
better than
anyone else

She called me names
she threatened me
this woman who now
murmurs to the plants
as she waters them

My hands
just washed
yet I
wash them again
after the news

Burial of a friend—
in spite of myself
I marvel at
the yellow butterfly
against the blue sky

The weather station says
spring begins at 3:58 p.m.
which is right now—
my reflection blurred
in the frozen puddle

Mother has sent
a photo of her facelift—
behind her an ancient
French cathedral
covered with scaffolding

Department meeting:
while the mouths utter business
the eyes ripple with
someone sailing, someone fishing
someone drowning

Today at work
I saw the complexity
of labor versus management—
a lake gull flies silently
throught the snowfall

If only years ago I
had seen myself more clearly—
the weight of many snowfalls
bends to the ground
the juniper branch

Kenneth Tanemura

Dad imprisoned
at Tule Lake . . .
now framed
in rosewood
decorating my room

the flower stand
at the train station
reminded me
I had no one
to buy flowers for

like receipts
of a business
gone bankrupt
I keep
these old love letters

writing a poem—
the cat
pushes
my pencil
with her nose

alone in a crowd:
even the seat
in this café
doesn't
fit

Brian Tasker

half awake
still dreaming
our legs entwined
around quarrels forgotten
in sleep

a dead friend
buried
deep within
the year's first dream
my forgotten grief

the wind-blown clouds
lighten and darken
lighten and darken
the room
in which we argue

my ex-wife
now pregnant
her belly tightens
the silver belt
that I gave her

late in the evening
the traffic sounds slowed
to a lull in the conversation . . .
she reaches for a cigarette
nothing else to tell me

long after she's left
the garden she tended
weeds reclaim the flowerbeds
my heart too
has grown wild

all day at my desk
to glance up
at sunset
the house bricks
a deeper red

whispered so quietly
the words of parting
I could hear
the cry of a kite
across the valley

hearing the news
and unable to find
any words of reply
only the beating
of the cursor on the screen

the hospital clerk hands me
my father's belongings
in a plastic bag
the familiar smell
of a ripening peach

Carolyn Thomas

just sitting
on this black cushion
there is nothing more

dawn at the east window
dusk at the west door

sleeping
on my lap
the cat
becomes a book-rest
for my other world

In the mist
the blue heron
slowly spreads its wings
and leaves behind the pond
as if it never was

when asked
after her own health

the silence
of this small bowl
of riverstones

turning leaves—
dressed in black
even the doll
seems ready
for the other world

Marc Thompson

nothing changes
when my father comes to visit
my wife and I
listen respectfully
mountains gathering snow

at two AM
on the night of the equinox
a little boy
sneaks out of the house
to play with the moon

on a Sunday night
at the end of the summer
an outdoor choir
sings the praises of Jesus
and longs for the end of the world

in 1917
Modigliani's model
smiled
knowing immortality
and youth

daffodils
come play with me
spring is
in the garden
and I must leave soon

Linda Jeannette Ward

lining the inner spine
of love poems you left
a frayed red thread
adhering as stubbornly
as your memory

a fine mist
drifting from stormy seas
touches my hair
with such a light caress
your hands once roused me

recovering from migraine
I doze fitfully on the beach
    a ghost crab
drags a bird's tiny skull
        into its hole

wildly flowing no more
the stream
we made love by
choked
by storm-torn limbs

paint me blurred
like a Monet garden
where imperfections fade
into lilacs and lilies
and autumn leaves never fall

after that stormy night
the Hospice Sister's
soft step in my room—
rain cradled
in a petal of magnolia

she jimmies a knife
beneath their wedding photo
tiny worm holes
have eroded
the rubber cement

after Mother's death
half-sister sorts photographs—
her childhood and mine
neatly divided
into separate piles of Dads

my arms around you as if
it would stop your dying
. . . on the edge of our worn trail
    half a hoof clings
    to a deer's leg bone

Michael Dylan Welch

this is but a moonless night,
and my pillow has no tear stains—
it is in the grocery aisle
amid the frozen vegetables
that I long for you

all my books collect dust
except the one of love poems
you gave me that day
when the spring rains
kept us indoors

the way you look at me
while I rub your arms—
you are the painting
I have never painted
a thousand times

jingle of the dog's collar
out in the hall—
we pause
in our lovemaking,
Christmas Eve

doing laundry
after the argument—
for a moment
she holds his best shirt
by the collar

her plane disappears
into starlight . . .
and somewhere
in her luggage
my love poem

a book on Hiroshima—
in the picture
of survivors
the one man
with closed eyes

two cars backing up
towards each other
in the clinic parking lot—
is this, like the morning's diagnosis,
what the future holds?

freeway empty
on Christmas morning—
the space
where the skid marks
change direction

I tell her I grow old
have a paunch and need new clothes
that the wild geese have flown
and winter is approaching
—my mother laughs

my pen poised
above the notepaper—
no words come
for my friend
moving away

this cold lonely night
without you, with no chance
of seeing you again,
how I wish
I could turn off the moon

you would not sleep on the pillow
I shared with a previous lover—
would you come now,
now that I have
a hundred new pillows

a snail has left
its delicate silver trail
on my book of love poems
left out on your porch
overnight

These words I write
Again and again—
Nothing in them adequately reveals
Knowledge or emotion,
And yet again I write them

Alison Williams

words
I never said
to you
the song of a bird
in a bitter wind

a ring
around the moon
tonight
missing something that
was never mine

closing
the bedroom window
to keep out
the new coolness
I turn on the radio

watching
the storm tossed trees
through glass
afraid to let myself go
where the wind would take me

older now
I dream that you still
sing to me
and that I write
poems for you

Paul O. Williams

the alarm goes off
at 5 a.m. to let him
catch a plane. He groans
through dressing, but what
a sunrise! What a sunrise!

after midnight
a distant motorcycle
blasts up the hill—
I will try to be grateful
for all that verve

It is time again
for migration—swallows
gather on the wires—
and what have I done this year
that anyone would notice?

Jeff Witkin

into the reeds
the duck's wake
slowly slips
and around the bend
all desire

in a curve of light
the crash and spray
of the full-moon tide;
   for a moment with arms crossed
   the power of my youth

after
she touches the sea
she turns to touch it again
except for this i am
unmoved all day

Karina Young

Taking a break
at midday
at times I take flight
with them, the birds
over the hill

Moonlight
through the blinds
the heat
of your hands
all over me

New vines spread
out along the wall
they did not bother
to tell you
it might come back

Dying sea lion
my decision
to let it be
wave after wave
in its eyes

It seems
you never went away
and I gave
your ashes
to the lonely sea
(for Carlota John Young, 1942-1996)

Poets' Biographies

ai li (b. Malaya; res. London, England; British) is the founding editor of *still: a journal of short verse* (1997-2001) and the online journal *dew-on-line*. A Fellow of the Royal Photographic Society, she lives in London's Belsize Park in two converted Victorian stables.

Kay F. Anderson (b. 1934; res. Redwood City, California; American) grew up hiking trails of Chief Blackhawk and his tribe between the Mississippi and Rock Rivers. A widely-published freelance writer, she later became internationally published and honored as a haiku, senryu, tanka, haibun and haiga poet. Her ordeal with advanced malignant melanoma led her to be commissioned to exhibit and paint sumi-e for a newly opened 'Healing with Hope' cancer clinic in San Mateo, California.

Fay Aoyagi (b. 1956 Tokyo, Japan; res. San Francisco, California; American) began writing English-language tanka in 1995. She won First Prize in the San Francisco International Tanka Contest 1997.

Pamela A. Babusci (b. 1950 Rochester, New York; res. Rochester, New York; American) has been writing tanka since 1994 and has been published in the USA, Canada, England, Japan, Australia and New Zealand. She received Tanka Splendor Awards in 1995-1999, 2001 and 2002, and was awarded First Place in the *Yellow Moon* Tanka Competition 2002.

John Barlow (b. 1970 Davenham, England; res. Liverpool, England; British) is the founding editor of *Tangled Hair*, the first journal dedicated to contem-porary English-language tanka to be published outside the US. He is also the editor of *The Haiku Calendar* and the haiku magazine *Snapshots*, and co-editor of *The New Haiku* (Snapshot Press, 2002). His own poems have received several international awards, and he has published three collections with Snapshot Press: *Flamingo Shapes* (2001) (haiku), *Snow About To Fall* (2003) (tanka), and *Waiting for the Seventh Wave* (2003) (haiku). He works as a design studio manager.

Marianne Bluger (b. 1945 Ottawa, Ontario, Canada; res. Ottawa, Ontario, Canada; Canadian) has published eight volumes of poetry, including *Gusts* (Penumbra Press, 1998)—the first book-length collection of tanka published in Canada—and *Early Evening Pieces, New and Selected Haiku* (Buschek Books, 2003). She received the Archibald Lampman Award for Poetry in 1993.

Janice M. Bostok (b. 1942 Mullumbimby, New South Wales, Australia; res. Dungay, New South Wales, Australia; Australian) has been writing haiku and tanka since 1971. She won first Place in the *Yellow Moon* Tanka Competition 1998, and received Tanka Spendor Awards in 1997 and 1998. She has published two collections of tanka, *Dimmed the Mystery* (Snapshot Press, 2000), and *Reaching Out From Dreaming* (self-published, 2001) along with many volumes of haiku and prose.

Naomi Y. Brown (b. 1920 Saitama Prefecture, Japan; res. Sun City West, Arizona; American) started writing tanka in Japanese as a high school and college student, and now writes both tanka and haiku in Japanese and English. She has published two collections of haiku, Seasons' Enigma (Yucca Books, 1988), and Haiku Tapestry (Yucca Books, 1996). She is currently a member of the Japanese-language tanka group 'California Tanka Kai'.

Marjorie Buettner (b. 1951 Bismarck, North Dakota; res. Minneapolis, Minnesota; American) has received numerous awards for her poetry, including First Place in the Haiku Society of America's Harold G. Henderson Award 2002, and a Tanka Splendor Award in 2001. She is a reviewer for *North Stone Review, Modern Haiku*, and *World Haiku Review.*

Margaret Chula (b. 1947 Brattleboro, Vermont; res. Portland, Oregon; American) is a poet, teacher, and performer. Her first haiku collection, *Grinding my ink* (Katsura Press, 1993), received First Place in the Haiku Society of America's Merit Book Awards 1994. She has published four further collections: *This Moment* (Katsura Press, 1995) (haiku), *Shadow Lines* (Katsura Press, 1995) (haibun, with Rich Youmans), *Always Filling, Always Full* (White Pine Press, 2001) (tanka), and *The Smell of Rust* (Katsura Press, 2003) (haiku).

Tom Clausen (b. 1951 Ithaca, New York; res. Ithaca, New York; American) graduated from Cornell University in 1973 and now works there in the A. R. Mann Library. He has published five collections, including *A Work of Love* (Tiny Poems Press, 1997) (tanka), and *Homework* (Snapshot Press, 2000) (tanka, haiku and senryu).

Gerard John Conforti (b. 1948 New York, New York; res. Staten Island, New York; American) was born to an alcoholic father and an emotionally ill mother, and from the age of four spent his childhood in the Mount Loretto orphanage on Staten Island. His collections include *Now that the Night Ends* (AHA Books/Chant Press, 1996) (tanka), *Pale Moonlight* (Deep North Press, 1999) (haiku), *For My Brother Victor & Elsa His Wife* (AHA Books, 2000) (tanka), and *Spirits of the Wind* (AHA Books, 2002) (tanka).

Geoffrey Daniel (b. 1955 Bedford, England; res. Dollar, Scotland; British) has lived in England, Malaysia, and East and Central Africa, and currently teaches in Scotland. His collection of haiku and tanka, *Gripping the Perch*, was published by Snapshot Press in 1998.

Cherie Hunter Day (b. 1954 Morristown, New Jersey; res. San Diego, California; American) trained as a biologist and worked as a researcher in field biology, molecular biology and genetics. She began writing haiku in the early 1970s, and tanka in 1993. She has published two collections of tanka: *Sun, Moon, Mother, Father* (Sundog Press, 1997), and the award-winning *Early Indigo* (Snapshot Press, 2000).

Melissa Dixon (b. 1923, Winnipeg, Canada; res. Victoria, British Columbia, Canada; Canadian) worked as an actor for forty years, and as a broadcaster and journalist under the name Peg Dixon in Winnipeg, Toronto, and Victoria. She has won tanka awards in Japan and North America.

Patricia Donegan (b. 1945, Chicago, Illinois; res. Tokyo, Japan; American) is a poet/writer teaching at a university in Tokyo, and a contributing editor for *Kyoto*. She is the recipient of a Fulbright Grant, and includes among her publications *Chiyo-ni: Woman Haiku Master* (Tuttle, 1998), and the collections *Without Warning, Hot Haiku* and *Heralding the Milk Light*.

Jeanne Emrich (b. 1947 Minneapolis, Minnesota; res. Edina, Minnesota; American) is a poet and artist, and the founder of *HAIGA Online: A Journal of Painting and Poetry*. She is the author of *The Haiku Habit* (Lone Egret Press, 1996), *Barely Dawn* (Lone Egret Press, 2000), and *Reeds: Contemporary Haiga* (Lone Egret Press, 2003);

and co-author (with Michael Dylan Welch) of *Berries and Cream: Contemporary Haiga in North America* (Press Here, 2000). Her manual, *The Haiku Habit Workshop Manual* (Lone Egret Press, 1998), is included in educational materials sent out to teachers by the Haiku Society of America.

Amelia Fielden (b. 1941 Sydney, Australia ; res. Newcastle, New South Wales, Australia; Australian) recently retired from service as a Japanese translator with the Australian government. She has published four books: *Eucalypts and Iris Streams* (Ginnindera Press, 2002), a bilingual collection of free verse, tanka and haiku; *On Tsukuba Peak* (Five Islands Press, 2002), English translations of tanka by Hatsue Kawamura; *Fountains Play and Time Passes* (Ginnindera Press, 2002), bilingual tanka with Yuko Kawano; and *Short Songs* (Ginnindera Press, 2003), prose featuring English-language tanka.

Stanford M. Forrester (b. 1963 Staten Island, New York; res. Wethersfield, Connecticut; American) edits *bottle rockets: a collection of short verse*, and *Unrolling the Awning: An Anthology from the Grand Central Station Tanka Café Group* (bottle rockets press, 2003). He served as president of the Haiku Society of America in 2003.

Garry Gay (b. 1951 Glendale, California; res. Windsor, California; American) has been a professional photographer since receiving his B.P.A. degree in photography in 1974. He is one of the co-founders of the Haiku Poets of Northern California, serving as their first president from 1989-1990, and again in 2001-2002. In 1991 he was elected president of the Haiku Society of America, and in the same year he co-founded Haiku North America. He also co-founded the American Haiku Archives in Sacramento, California. His haiku collections include *The Billboard Cowboy* (Smythe-Waithe Press, 1982), *The Silent Garden* (Smythe-Waithe Press, 1982), *Wings Of Moonlight* (Smythe-Waithe Press, 1993), *River Stones* (Saki Press, 1999), and *Along The Way* (Snapshot Press, 2000).

Sanford Goldstein (b. 1925 Cleveland, Ohio; res. Niigata City, Japan; American) is Professor Emeritus of Purdue University and of Keiwa College in Japan. He received an Arts Literature Program Fellowship from the National Endowment for the Arts for his co-translation of Mokichi Saito's *Red Lights*. His co-translations of other works of Japanese literature include Akiko Yosano's *Tangled Hair: Selected Tanka from Midaregami* (Purdue University Studies, 1971; revised edition Cheng & Tsui, 2002), *Takuboku Ishikawa's Sad Toys* Tuttle, 1985), *Shiki Masaoka's Songs From a Bamboo Village* (Tuttle, 1998), and *Ryokan: Selected Tanka & Haiku* (Kokodo, 2000). He has also published four collections of his own tanka: *This Tanka World, Gaijin Aesthetics* , *At the Hut of the Small Mind, Records of a Well-Polished Satchel #7: 14 Occasional Poems* and most recently *This Tanka Whirl* in 2001.

LeRoy Gorman (b. 1949 Smiths Falls, Ontario, Canada; res. Napanee, Ontario, Canada; Canadian) teaches in Kingston. He has published numerous collections of haiku and visual poetry, including *glass bell* (King's Road Press, 1991) and *nothing personal* (proof press, 2001). He edits Haiku Canada Publications, and publishes under his pawEpress imprint.

Caroline Gourlay (b. 1939 London, England; res. Knighton, Wales; British) has lived all her married life in the Welsh Border country where she and her farmer husband brought up their three sons. She has published four collections of poetry: *Crossing The Field* (Redlake Press, 1995) (haiku), *Reading All Night* (Hub Editions, 1999) (haiku and tanka), *Through the Café Door* (Snapshot Press, 2000) (haiku), and *Against the Odds* (Hub Editions, 2001) (haiku). She edited *Blithe Spirit, Journal of the British Haiku Society* from 1998-2000, and is currently a Patron of the Ledbury Poetry Society.

Yvonne Hardenbrook (b. 1928 Hot Springs, Virginia; res. Columbus, Ohio; American) is a retired teacher and journalist. Her publications include the haiku collection *saying enough* (Amelia, 1989), and *Greatest Hits* (Pudding House, 2001). Her tanka have appeared in several anthologies and journals, and have won awards in the US, England and Japan.

Christopher Herold (b. 1948 Suffern, New York; res. Port Townsend, Washington; American) was a professional percussionist for many years, and is now a lay Zen Buddhist monk and the managing editor of *The Heron's Nest,* a monthly journal of haiku. His haiku collection *A Path in the Garden* (Katsura Press, 2000) received a Haiku Society of America Merit Book Award in 2001. His other books are *In Other Words* (Jarus Books, 1981) (haiku), *Coincidence* (Kanshiketsu Press, 1987) (haiku), *Voices of Stone* (Kanshiketsu Press, 1995) (haibun), and *In the Margins of the Sea* (Snapshot Press, 2000) (haiku and tanka).

Jeanne Jorgensen (b. 1943 Abee, Alberta, Canada; res. Edmonton, Alberta, Canada; Canadian) was born in a two-room cabin on a farm in Northern Alberta, and started writing poetry at the age of eight. Her collections include *New Kid on the Block* (Four Seasons Corner, 1990) (haiku and senryu), *Border Crossing: haiku and related poetry* (Four Seasons Corner, 1993), *And So It Was* (Four Seasons Corner, 1998) (tanka), and *Briefly Snowflakes* (King's Road Press, 2001) (haiku).

Jim Kacian (b. 1953 Worcester, Massachusetts, res. Winchester, Virginia; American) is the author of eight books, editor of many more, owner of Red Moon Press and a co-founder of the World Haiku Association. He has served as editor of *Frogpond*, the international journal of the Haiku Society of America, since 1998.

kirsty karkow (b. 1937 London, England; res. Waldoboro, Maine; American) has at times been a competitive dressage rider, an instructor in t'ai chi, and a sculptor in stone and clay. Her tanka have been published in the US, Canada, England and Japan, and she received a Tanka Splendor Award in 2001.

Doris Kasson (b. 1925 Petersburg, Nebraska; res. Belleair Bluffs, Florida; American) has spent most of her adult life packing and unpacking in moves around the globe with her family. She received Tanka Splendor Awards in 2000 and 2001.

Michael Ketchek (b. 1954 Detroit, Michigan; res. Rochester, New York; American) is a day-care teacher by day, and a baseball fan/poet by night.

Larry Kimmel (b. 1940 Johnstown, Pennsylvania; res. Colrain, Massachusetts; American) holds degrees from Oberlin Conservatory and Pittsburgh University. He has published a novel, *A Small Silent Ordeal* (Aegina Press, 1993), and six collections with Winfred Press: *alone tonight* (1998) (haiku & tanka), *the necessary fly* (2001) (haiku), *the inadequacy of long-stemmed roses* (2001) (cherita), *Cold Stars White Moon* (2002) (tanka), *As Far As Thought Can Reach* (2002) (tanka & prose poems), and *a spill of apples* (2003) (tanrenga with Carol Purington).

Robert Kusch (b. 1934 Evanston, Illinois; res. New Brunswick, New Jersey; American) teaches American Literature at Rutgers University. He began writing tanka in the early 1990s.

Leatrice Lifshitz (b. 1933 New York, New York; d. 2003 Pomona, New York; American) received several awards for her tanka and haiku, including a Tanka Splendor Award in 1994 and First Place in the Haiku Society of America's Harold G. Henderson Award 1997.

Geraldine Clinton Little (b. 1923 Portstewart, Northern Ireland; d. 1997 Mt. Holly, New Jersey; American) was a poet, writer, singer and educator. Her volumes of poetry and fiction won numerous awards, including the prestigious PEN award for Short Fiction, and she published several collections of haiku and tanka, including *More Light, Larger Vision* (AHA Books, 1992). A long-time professor of English and Poetry at the Burlington County College, she served as president of the Haiku Society of America, as well as vice president of the Poetry Society of America, in the 1980s.

Martin Lucas (b. 1962 Middlesbrough, England; res. Preston, England; British) is the co-editor of *The Iron Book of British Haiku* (Iron Press, 1998) and *The New Haiku* (Snapshot Press, 2002), and the editor of the haiku magazine, *Presence*, which regularly features tanka. His PhD thesis, 'Haiku in Britain', included sections on tanka and its relation to haiku.

Laura Maffei (b. 1967 Brooklyn, New York; res. Staten Island, New York; American) is the founding editor of *American Tanka*, currently the only US literary journal devoted exclusively to contemporary English-language tanka. She began writing tanka in 1992 after reading translations of Yosano Akiko and Tawara Machi, and founded the journal in 1996 while working as a contract technical writer for the Texas state government. She currently teaches literature at Wagner College and St John's University.

Thelma Mariano (b. 1952 Montreal, Quebec, Canada; res. Montreal, Quebec, Canada; Canadian) has published two collections of tanka, *Night Sky* (self-published, 2000), and *On Such a Night* (The Wooden Basement Press, 2001). She works as a life coach, personal growth columnist, and writer of contemporary women's fiction.

Michael McClintock (b. 1950 Los Angeles, California; res. South Pasadena, California; American) edits *The New American Imagist* for Hermitage West, and is the consulting and contributing editor for *Journeys: A Quarterly of English-language Haibun*. He also writes the 'Tanka Café' column for the *Tanka Society of America Newsletter*, and numerous reviews and essays for magazines and journals devoted to haiku, related literature, and the short poem. His early collections of poetry include *Light Run* (Shiloh, 1971) (haiku/senryu) and *Man With No Face* (Shelters Press, 1974) (tanka). A collection of haibun, *Anthology of Days*, appeared (Backwoods Broadsides) in 2002. His work has appeared in each edition of *The Haiku Anthology* (Doubleday-Anchor, 1974; Simon & Schuster, 1986; W. W. Norton, 1999).

anne mckay (b. 1932 Ottawa, Ontario; d. 2003 Vancouver, British Columbia; Canadian) published twenty collections of poetry during her lifetime, including *sometimes in a certain light* (1985), *in the house of winter* (1987), *come at nine come at nine* (1994), and *a matter of wings* (1996)—all from Wind Chimes Press—and *A capella: poems selected and new* (Cacanadadada Press, 1994).

Lenard D. Moore (b. 1958 Jacksonville, North Carolina; res. Jacksonville, North Carolina; American) is a poet, fiction writer, freelance writer, cultural arts consultant, lecturer, arts administrator, and literary critic. He has published three books, including *The Open Eye* (self-published, 1985) and *Forever Home* (St Andrews College Press, 1992). He currently teaches at Shaw University.

Matt Morden (b. 1962 Usk, Wales; res. Hermon, Wales; British) received Tanka Splendor Awards in 2000, 2001, and 2002. His first haiku collection, *A Dark Afternoon*, was published in 2000 by Snapshot Press, and his work also features in *A New Resonance 2: Emerging Voices in English-Language Haiku* (Red Moon Press, 2001). He is the associate editor of *Snapshots*.

June Moreau (b. 1933 Waltham, Massachusetts; res. Lexington, Massachusetts; American) has received numerous awards for her poetry, including a Penumbra Haiku Award in 2000. Her most recent book is *just enough light: Haiku and Tanka* (Koyama Press, 2002).

Pamela Miller Ness (b. 1951 Boston, Massachusetts; res. New York, New York; American) currently teaches English at The Dalton School, New York, and haiku workshops for teachers at the Japan Society. She has served as vice president and chair of the Education Committee for The Haiku Society of America, newsletter editor for the Tanka Society of America, and chair of the organizing committee for Haiku North America 2003. Her haiku and tanka have appeared in numerous international journals and anthologies, and she won First Prize in the San Francisco International Tanka Contest 2001. Her publications include two tanka collections from Swamp Press: *Alzheimer's Waltz* (1999), and *Like Salt on Sun Spray* (2001).

Francine Porad (b. 1929 Seattle, Washington; res. Bellevue, Washington; American) served as president of the Haiku Society of America from 1993-1995. A painter and poet, her collections of haiku and tanka include *Connections* (1986), *A Mural of Leaves* (1991), and *The Perfect Worry-Stone* (2000), all from Vandina Press.

Carol Purington (b. 1949 Colrain, Massachusetts; res. Colrain, Massachusetts; American) lives on a dairy farm in Western Massachusetts. She has published five books, including two collections of haiku, a volume of haiku-related works, and two tanka-influenced narratives: *The Trees Bleed Sweetness* (1997), and *A Pattern for This Place* (2001). She received First Prize in the Tanka Society of America's International Tanka Contest 2002.

218

William M. Ramsey (b. 1945 Bethlehem, Pennsylvania; res. Florence, South Carolina; American) has written haiku, haibun, and tanka over the last decade. His book of haiku, *This Wine*, was published in 2002 by Deep North Press.

Jane Reichhold (b. 1937 Lima, Ohio; res. Gualala, California; American) published early English-language tanka in her magazine, *Mirrors International Haiku Forum*, and founded the Tanka Splendor Awards in 1990. Since 1993 she has co-edited *Lynx: A Journal for Linking Poets*, and she is also the co-editor of *Wind Five Folded* (AHA Books, 1994), the first international anthology of English-language tanka. Her own books of tanka include *A Gift of Tanka* (1990), *In the Presence* (1998) (with Werner Reichhold), and *Geography Lens* (1999), all from AHA Books. She is also the translator, with Hatsue Kawamura, of *White Letter Poems by Fumi Saito* (AHA Books, 1998), *Heavenly Maiden Tanka by Akiko Baba* (AHA Books, 1999), and *A String of Flowers, Untied . . . Love Poems from The Tale of Genji by Murasaki Shikibu* (Stone Bridge Press, 2003).

David Rice (b. 1945 New York, New York; res. Berkeley, California; American) works as a psychologist in private practice. His tanka have appeared in journals and anthologies since 1991, and he has self-published two chapbooks of tanka sequences: *In Each Other's Footsteps* (1996) and *My California* (2002). He has a particular interest in writing tanka sequences with other poets, two of which, written with Cherie Hunter Day, received Tanka Splendor Awards in 2000 and 2001.

Edward J. Rielly (b. 1943 Darlington, Wisconsin; res. Westbrook, Maine; American) chairs the English Department at St Joseph's College of Maine. His eight books of poetry include five collections of haiku and an online collection of tanka, *How Sky Holds the Sun* (AHA Books, 1998). He has also published several cultural history books, including *Baseball: An Encyclopedia of Popular Culture* (ABC-CLIO, 2000), *The 1960s* (Greenwood, 2003), and *Baseball and American Culture: Across the Diamond* (Haworth, 2003). He received First Prize in the Tanka Society of America's International Tanka Contest 2001.

Alexis K. Rotella (b. 1947 Johnstown, Pennsylvania; res. Arnold, Maryland; American) is a licensed acupuncturist and bioenergetic medicine consultant. A former president of the Haiku Society of America, her work has appeared in numerous journals and anthologies, and has received several awards.

Philip Rowland (b. 1970 Twickenham, England; res. Tokyo, Japan; British) works as a lecturer in the Department of International Studies at Tamagawa University.

Elizabeth St Jacques (b. 1939 Iroquois Falls, Ontario, Canada; res. Sault Ste. Marie, Ontario, Canada;

Canadian) has been published in numerous journals and anthologies, and is a regular reviewer for *Frogpond*, *Haiku Canada Newsletter*, and *Lynx*. She is the editor and webmaster of *Poetry In The Light*.

Gerald St. Maur (b. London, England; res. Edmonton, Alberta, Canada; Canadian) has been a student of Japanese poetic forms ever since a visit to Honshu and Hokkaido in 1974, and he occasionally lectures on these forms in the Department of East Asian Studies at the University of Alberta. His haiku and tanka are widely anthologized, and he edited the tanka anthology *Countless Leaves* (Inkling Press, 2001). He works as a writer and visual artist.

Pat Shelley (b. 1910 San Jose, California; d. 1996 Saratoga, California; American) worked as a librarian, specializing in poetry, children's literature, and story-telling. A poet and artist, she served as tanka editor for *Woodnotes* and published three poetry collections during her lifetime: *As I Go* (1976), *Glass Eye* (1982), and *The Rice Papers* (1992). A posthumous collection of tanka, *Turning My Chair*, was published by Press Here in 1997.

Ruby Spriggs (b. 1929 Leicester, England; d. 2001 Ottawa, Ontario, Canada; British/Canadian) emigrated to Canada in 1957 and began her writing career in 1970. Her work has been published in leading international journals and anthologies, and has earned numerous awards. She served as editor of *Haiku Canada Newsletter* from 1990-92, and as coeditor of *RAW NerVZ* in 1994. Her own collections include *Sunshadow/Moonshadow* (Heron's Cave, 1986), and *Switching Off the Shadows* (King's Road Press, 1996).

Art Stein (b. 1928 Brooklyn, New York; res. Northfield, Massachusetts; American) is an architect and equestrian. He placed second in the Tanka Society of America's International Tanka Contest 2002.

John Stevenson (b. 1948 Ithaca, New York; res. Nassau, New York; American) is a former president of the Haiku Society of America, and has served as Associate Editor of its journal, *Frogpond*, since 2002. His collections include *Something Unerasable* (self-published, 1996) (haiku), and *Some of the Silence* (Red Moon Press, 1999) (haiku and tanka).

George Swede (b. 1940 Riga, Latvia; res. Toronto, Ontario, Canada; Canadian) has published thirty collections of poetry, the most recent being *Almost Unseen: Selected Haiku of George Swede* (Brooks Books, 2000). He has also edited seven anthologies, including *Global Haiku: Twenty-five Poets World-wide* (Mosaic Press/ Iron Press, 2000), and published numerous other books. His tanka have appeared in several of the major English-language tanka publications as well as in several of his collections. He lives part of the year in a small Mexican town.

Kenneth Tanemura (b. 1970 Redwood City, California; res. Queens, New York; American) co-founded the first American English-language tanka magazine, *Five Lines Down*, with Sanford Goldstein. He has published two collections of tanka and haiku: *No Love Poems* (Small Poetry Press, 1993), and *This Tanka World of Strings* (Small Poetry Press, 1994). He is currently an associate editor for *Monolid: A Magazine for Asian Americans Who Aren't Blinking*.

Brian Tasker (b. 1949 London, England; res. Frome, England; British) founded and edited the poetry journal *Bare Bones* (1992-1995). He has published five collections of haiku with Bare Bones Press: *notes from a humdrum* (1992), *housebound in nirvana* (1992), *woodsmoke* (1993), *a ragbag of haiku* (1994), and *the sound of rain* (1999). His collection of tanka, *the wind-blown clouds*, appeared from the same publisher in 1996. He is also the editor of *In the ship's wake* (Iron Press, 2001), an anthology of contemporary English-language tanka.

Carolyn Thomas (b. 1952 Napa, California; res. Cathedral City, California; American) is a painter and poet. She has been writing haiku for over twenty years, and has published several books in this genre, but only recently began to write tanka.

Marc Thompson (b. 1949 Schenectady, New York; res. Minneapolis, Minnesota; American) has been writing tanka since 1996. A computer consultant by trade, he is currently pursuing a master's degree in creative and critical writing.

Linda Jeannette Ward (b. 1947 Washington, District of Columbia; res. Coinjock, North Carolina; American) has published two collections of her work: *a frayed red thread* (Clinging Vine Press, 2000) (tanka), and *a delicate dance of wings* (Winfred Press/Clinging Vine Press, 2002) (haibun). She is also the editor of *Full Moon Tide: The Best of Tanka Splendor 1990-1999* (Clinging Vine Press, 2000).

Michael Dylan Welch (b. 1962 Watford, England; res. Sammamish, Washington; British/Canadian) founded the Tanka Society of America in 2000, and is currently serving as the group's president. From 1989-1997 he edited *Woodnotes*, and in early 1994 was the editor of *Footsteps in the Fog* (Press Here), which was perhaps the first anthology of tanka written in the English language. He has won First Prize in each of the Henderson, Brady, and Drevniok haiku and senryu contests, and First Prize in the San Francisco International Tanka Contest 1999. He is also the editor and publisher of *Tundra: The Journal of the Short Poem*, and of Press Here books.

Alison Williams (b. 1957 Sleaford, England; res. Southampton, England; British) had her first tanka published in 1999. She received Tanka Splendor Awards in 2000 and 2002.

Paul O. Williams (b. 1935 Chatham, New Jersey; res. Belmont, California; American) is a retired English professor. He served as president of the Haiku Society of America in 1999, and has published *Outside Robins Sing: Selected Haiku* (Brooks Books, 2000), and a book of haiku criticism, *The Nick of Time* (Press Here, 1999).

Jeff Witkin (b. 1953 Washington, District of Columbia; res. Carmel, Indiana; American) has published two books of haiku and tanka: *the duck's wake* (self-published, 1996), and *Beyond Where the Snow Falls* (Tiny Poems Press, 1997).

Karina Young (b. 1969 Augusta, Maine; res. Salinas, California; American) is the newsletter editor for the Haiku Poets of Northern California, and supports herself as an editor at CTB/McGraw-Hill. Her tanka collection, *Bursts of Flight*, was published in 2000 by Vines of Light Press.

(John Barlow's assistance was essential in preparing the preceding biographies and is greatly appreciated. Dee Evetts' expert proofreading of this volume was likewise invaluable.)

Acknowledgments

Acknowledgments

The editors thank the following poets, journals, and publishers for permission to print these poems. In most cases, additional information about magazines, books, and other sources cited below may be found in the bibliographies following the Introduction or in the Biographical Notes. Book titles are shown below in italics.

Abbreviations used:

AHA:	AHA Books, Gualala, CA
AT:	*American Tanka*
BS:	*Blithe Spirit*
FLD:	*Five Lines Down*
FP:	*Frogpond*
HPNC:	Haiku Poets of Northern California
HSA:	Haiku Society of America
PR:	*Presence*
RN:	*RAW NerVZ Haiku*
SN:	*Snapshots*
ST:	*still*
TH:	*Tangled Hair*
TSA:	Tanka Society of America
WFF:	*Wind Five Folded*
WHR:	*World Haiku Review*
WN:	*Woodnotes*
YM:	*Yellow Moon*

ai li: "river rain" *The Art of Haiku 2000*, ed. Gerald England, New Hope International, 2000; "on that night train" *RN* VI:3; "i find a lake" and "reading you" *ST3* four; "at twilight" *AT* #8; "the last train" *AT* #6; "moonlight" *AT* #4. **Anderson**: "Gone wandering" *Brussels Sprout* XII:2; "You say this" *WN* #23. **Aoyagi**: "Indian summer" *TH* #2; "a farmer's market" *AT* #4; "a tofu shop is gone" *Lynx* XII:1; "spring equinox" *Tanka Splendor* Award 1996;"my father" *WN* #30; "cherry blossom storm" *Tanka Splendor* Award 1998; "the names etched" *ST4* Four; "a first kiss" *RN* VII:3; "passing a maternity dress shop" first prize, HPNC Tanka Contest 1997; "passing the artichoke fields" *RN* VIII:1. **Babusci**: "i am" *FLD*; "scattered lovers" *ST5* two, runner up Spring 2001 competition; "fastening" first prize Tanka Award *Yellow*

Moon Competition 2002; "i remove my cross" *FP* XVIII:3; "not a single star" *Tanka Splendor* Award 1999. **Barlow:** "dawn" *PR* #13; "summer" *SN* #3 (July 1998); "the way you are sleeping" *Lynx* XIII:2; "away from home" *AT* #6; "sitting alone" *AT* #7; "hours" *AT* #1; "you talk on the phone" *BS* 8:2; "just five minutes: *Lynx* XV:1; "snow" *BS* 9:4; "in the dark" *In the Ship's Wake*; "a quiet moment" *Lynx* XVI:1; "together at last" first prize, *Yellow Moon* International Tanka Competition 2000; "unexpectedly" *Tanka Splendor* Award 2000; "something missing" *Tanka Splendor* Award 2002. **Bluger:** "turning" *AT* #10; "on our way" *The Tanka Journal* #20; "real" *The Tanka Journal* #18; "through midnight rain" *AT* #8; all other poems from *Gusts* (Penumbra Press, 1998). **Bostok:** "the sky becomes" & "beginning" *Hearing the Wind*, 1976; "awake" *Reaching Out From Dreaming*, 2001; "in half sleep" *TH* #1. **Brown:** "red mushroom" *WFF*; "no one" *FLD* 1996. **Buettner:** "this morning" *Woodpecker* VI:1; "vacation's end" *ST* V:2; "late summer" *WHC Review* November 2001; "spring rain" *TH* #3. **Chula:** "after the cease fire" first prize, The Japan Tanka Poets' Society International English Tanka Contest 2000; "my friends tell me" & "the black negligee" *Always Filling, Always Full* (White Pine Press, 2001); "how old are you now" Third Place, HPNC Contest 2001. **Clausen:** "every few bounces" *WFF*; "she's not here" *Mirrors* February 1995; "I had it all" *FP* XVIII:4; "the house quiet" *WN* #28; "as I sit in thought" and "it occurs to me" *Homework* (Snapshot Press, 2000); "it's not for" *RN* V: 1; "between chores" *A Work of Love* (Tiny Poems Press, 1997); *Homework*; "quite by surprise" *Tanka Splendor* Award 1998; "my beer gone flat" and "as useless" *TH* #2. **Conforti:** "On this autumn day" *Now That the Night Ends* (AHA Books and Chant Press, 1996); "every day that passes" www.ahapoetry.com/conforbk.htm. **Daniel:** "I built that wall" and "ebbtide—the dinghies" *Gripping the Perch* (Snapshot Press, 1998); "it is a pale horse" *WFF*; "was there ever" *TH* #1. **Day:** "watching" *AT* #6; "a long lunch" *AT* #3; "the music box" *Hummingbird* X:3; "flash of white" *TH* #2; "waiting past midnight" *AT* #11; "you asked" *Early Indigo* (Snapshot Press, 2000); "through patterned glass" *AT* #12; "far more often" *Lynx* XIII:3; "news of his death" *Tanka Splendor* Award 1997; "clear night, owl night" *TH* #3; "returning" *Lynx* XII:1. **Dixon:** "shimmering shapes" *Lynx* XV:3; "low slow breathing" Third Prize, The Japan Tanka Poets' Society International English Tanka Contest 2000; "the secluded park" *Tanka Splendor* Award 2000. **Donegan:** "will I know the last moment" *Bone Poems* (Chinook Press, 1985); "Tonight," *Without Warning* (Parallax Press 1996). **Emrich:** "dry seeds scatter" *Tanka Splendor* Award 1998; "old pine" *AT* #5; "today my heart" *Tanka Splendor* Award 2000; "not thinking really" *AT* #11; "don't take me" *AT* #6. **Fielden:** "I wanted" *AT* #10; "halving fruit" *TSA Newsletter* II:1; "my father" *TH* #3. **Forrester:** "autumn clouds" & "i keep your memory" *THr* #3; "sitting, watching" *Haiku Presence* #17); "Coney Island boardwalk" *Castles in the Sand*. **Gay:** "Age spots" first prize, *Yellow Moon* Tanka Contest 1999; "You rise to leave" *Tanka Splendor* Award 1996; "A quick hug" *Countless Leaves*. **Goldstein:** "snow" & "tonight's" *Gaijin Aesthetics* (Juniper Press, 1983); "I am a lump" *At the Hut of the Small Mind* (AHA Books, 1992); "no red wheelbarrow" *Hummingbird* IV:1; "Buddha" *WFF*; "Anne Frank" *AT* #9; "at times, mother," "swept up," & "only a one-sentence" *This Tanka Whirl* (Clinging Vine Press, 2001); "frying" *ST* V:2; "lull me, muse," *The*

Tanka Journal #20. **Gourlay**: "the same room" & "after" *Reading All Night* (Hub Press, 1999); "watching you" *BS* XI:1; "sitting beside you" *Castles in the Sand*. **Hardenbrook**: "as you sit" *Lynx* XIII:2; "the blizzard" *Tundra* #2; "down on my knees" *Tanka Splendor* Award 1993; "facelift" 2nd honorable mention, HPNC Tanka Contest 1999; "you ask" 2nd Prize, HPNC Tanka Contest 1998. **Herold**: "high tide" *In the Margins of the Sea* (Snapshot Press, 2000); "in her convertible" & "in morning fog" *WFF*; "small umbrella" *Footsteps in the Fog*. **Jorgensen**: "your name and address" & "swallowing tears" *Tanka Splendor* Award 1990; "he's traveled" *RN* VII:4. **karkow**: "strong wind" *Lynx* XV:3; "torrid day" *TSA Newsletter* III:2; "december sunrise" *TH* #3. **Kasson**: "whenever i notice" *Tanka Splendor* Award 2000; "afterwards" Third Prize, America International Tanka Contest 2000; "they seem" *WHR* March 2002; "sundays she talks" & "he uses them" *AT* #10; "nestled together" *AT* #11; "invited at last" *Tanka Splendor* Award 2001; "calling her" *TSA Newsletter* III:2. **Ketchek**: "in the language" *TS* 2001; "her husband" *FLD* #4; "not having it all" *RN* IV:1; "carefully" *RN* V:2. **Kimmel**: "looking down" *Tanka Splendor* Award 1995; "around the campfire" *The Christian Science Monitor* 21 June 1996; "as twilight gathers" *The Christian Science Monitor* 30 August 1996; "for fifty years" *WN*#31; "when I think" *Tanka Splendor* Award 1999; "still angry" *ST* 3; "I'm just saying" *AT* #9; "touch—touch—" & "walking" *RN* VII:3. **Kusch**: "Tossing a stone" *AT* #10; "Lightning on" *AT* #11; "For a moment" *TS* 1994; "Past midnight" *Northwest Literary Forum* 19; "It wants us" *WFF*. **Lifshitz**: "writing" *TS* 1999; "a gravel road" *AT* #8 (Spring 2000); "all her things" *AT* #5. **Little**: all from *More Light, Larger Vision* (AHA Books, 1992). **Lucas**: "on Ascension Day", "awake past midnight", "hordes of sightseers", "damselflies" *darkness and light* (Hub Editions, 1996); "futile task" *BS* VI:3; "stuck for conversation" *TS* #1; "the rattle of hangers" *TH* #3; "the many night noises of London" *BS* VIII:1. **Maffei**: "energy waning" *Lynx* XIII:1; "the clock on the wall" & "in this crazy March" *Lynx* XII:1; "tucked away" & "ovulating" *The Tanka Journal* #19; "amid the jumping" *Mirrors International* IX; "from the confines" *Woodpecker* 3:1; "morning" *TH* #3; "as if she feels" 2nd Prize, The Japan Tanka Poets' Society International English Tanka Contest 2000. **Mariano**: "I am alone" *AT* #9; "years on my own" *Tanka Splendor* Award 2000; "the morning after" *Tanka Splendor* Award 2002. **McClintock**: "biting" *Man With No Face* (Shelters Press, 1974); "raindrops" *RN* VII:1; "carrying the sun, the clouds" *AT* #12; "next door" *AT* #9; "Yale-educated" *RN* VII:3; "the moon tonight" *AT* #13; "here's a guy" *The Haiku Anthology* (2nd ed., edited by Cor van den Heuvel, Simon & Schuster, 1986). **mckay**: "shopkeepers" *a capella* (Cacanadadada Press, 1994); all other tanka from *come at nine come at nine* (Wind Chimes Press, 1994). **Moore**: "glowing moon" *Tanka Splendor* Award 1994; "moon over the cottage" *Japanophile* XX:3; "Funeral Parlor" *WFF*; "grandma frying" *Catch the Fire: A Cross-Generational Anthology of Contemporary African-American Poetry* (Riverhead Books, 1998). **Morden**: "when I have died" *Tanka Splendor* Award 2000; "away from home" Winner, Spread the Word Poetry Postcard Competition, 2002. **Moreau**: "What's on the other side" *Heron Dance*; "sun-smoke rises" *Moondust* (Koyama Press); "scattering them" *TS*; "When the cello" & "it is woven" *WN*; "such a fine feeling" *Lynx*; "a green bowl" *Northwest Literary Forum*; "Rice pudding" *Hummingbird*.

Ness: "Dear May Sarton" *AT* #3; "After" *TH* #1; "Autumn," first prize, HPNC International Tanka Competition 2001; "Apart" *TH* #2; "November chill" *TH* #1; "Like Chagall's" *The Tanka Journal* #19); "Night" *TSA Newsletter* II:3. **Porad**: "some cathedrals" *Lynx* XI:; "morning sun" *Cicada* 1992; "Michaelangelo" first prize, The Japan Tanka Poets' Society International English Tanka Contest 1992; "photos fall" *FLD* #3; "I paint" *AT* #2; "a woman" *WN#22*; "inscrutable face" *Lynx* XI:2; "Mama" 2nd Prize, HWUP Tanka Contest 1992; "holding" & "I drop" Grand Prize, HWUP Tanka Contest 1993; "van with my mother" honorable mention HWUP Tanka Contest 1993. **Purington**: "Weeks isolated" *WFF*; "Her sharp knife quick" first prize, TSA International Tanka Contest 2000; "First picking" *The Christian Science Monitor,* 19 July 2001; "He returns at dusk" *A Pattern for this Place* (Winfred Press, 2001); "A dream blows away" Third Prize, TSA International Tanka Contest 2002; "Smell of narcissus" *Tanka Splendor* Award 1997; "The river runs away" *AT* #10; "The white bear that walks" *Lynx Online* May 2001; "Indigo bird" *Tanka Splendor* Award 2000. **Ramsey**: "a gnat's smudge" *Lynx* XV:3; "three girls" *AT* #8; "When i am gone" *Hummingbird* XI:1; "one day" *Lynx* XV:1 (2000); "floating there" *RN* VI:2; "this road" *AT* #9 (Fall 2000); "the hole" *AT* #11 (Fall 2001); "Where is it now" *Countless Leaves.* **Reichhold**: "in the pantry" *Geography Lens* (AHA Books, 1999); "hair clean and long" *AT* #1; all other tanka from *In the Presence*, Jane & Werner Reichhold, AHA Books, 1998. **Rice**: "mountain meadow" *FLD* Winter 1994; "spring cleaning" *WFF*; "after the storm" *HWUP!* #39 (1996); "you nap" *TH* #3 (2001). **Rielly**: "black hole", "beyond the stadium," & "my birdfeeder" *How Sky Holds the Sun* (AHA Books online, 1998); "traveling the path", first prize, *TSA* International Tanka Contest 2000; "first leaves fall" *Castles in the Sand.* **Rotella**: "New Year's Eve" *Tanka Splendor* Award 1992; all others from *The Lace Curtain (A Collection of Tanka)* (Jade Mountain Press, 1989). **Rowland**: "pre-dawn blackness" *Hummingbird* XI:3 (March 2001). **Shelley**: "I will give you" *The Rice Papers* (Saratoga Trunk, 1992); all other tanka from *Turning my Chair* (Press Here, 1997). **Spriggs**: "a sudden loud noise" *Countless Leaves*; "always too busy" *Tanka in English*, The Japan Tanka Poets' Society 3rd International Tanka Convention, 2000; "After Chemo" *Haiku Canada Newsletter* XII:1. **St Jacques**: "between snow spots" *Lynx* XVI:2; "in full bright light" *Tanka Splendor* Award 1995; "winding trail" *Lynx online* (September 2000). **St. Maur**: "Where has she gone to" *AT* #12; "On the left-hand page" *Castles in the Sand.* **Stein**: "my fingers" *AT* #7; "Each foot" *RN* VI:1; "the sun and" *Black Bough* #12; "news" *RN* VI:3; "through the fog" *AT* #13; "releasing" *RN* VI:2; "barefoot" *Countless Leaves*; "returning at dusk" 2nd Prize, TSA International Tanka Contest 2002. **Stevenson**: "June" *Castles in the Sand*; "so clear, years later" *RN* II:4; "the leaves" 2nd Prize, HPNC Tanka Contest 2001; "of course" *TSA Newsletter* III:2; "still a newcomer" honorable mention, HPNC Tanka Contest 2001; "autumn street" *Lynx* XII:2. **Swede**: "I re-read" *FP* VIII:2; "Last night I felt" Third Prize, Poetry Society of Japan 2nd International Tanka Contest 1990; "Side-by-side,""Writing a poem," & "Cold winter morning" *Tanka Splendor* Award 1991; "Up at the first" & "Crowded bar" *The Plaza* #1; "She called me names" *WFF*; "My hands" *Hummingbird* 4:2; "Burial of a friend" *Poets in the Classroom* (ed. by B. Struthers & S. Klassen, Pembroke, 1995); "The weather station says" *The Haiku Quarterly* #17; "Mother has sent" *AT* #5; "Department meeting" *The Tanka Journal* #14 (1999); "Today at work" *New Moon: An Introduction to Issues in Contemporary American Tanka, Acorn* Supplement #2, Fall 2001; "If only years ago I" *AT* #12 (2002). **Tanemura**: "Dad imprisoned" *Loop* I:1; "the flower stand" *AT* #2; "like receipts" & "writing a poem" *Footsteps in the Fog*; "alone in a crowd" *How To Haiku: A Writer's Guide to Haiku and Related Forms* (Bruce Ross, Tuttle, 2002). **Tasker**: "whispered so quietly" *PR* #7; "Hearing the news" *TH* #3; all other tanka from the *wind-blown clouds* (Bare Bones Press, 1996). **Thomas**: "when asked" *AT* #10; "In the mist" *Tundra* #2; "just sitting" & "turning leaves" *puddle on the ink stone: haiku and other short poems* (2003); "sleeping" *Castles in the Sand*. **Thompson**: "nothing changes" *AT* #2; "at two AM" *ST* 4:3; "on a Sunday night" *Lynx* XV:3. **Ward**: "lining the inner spine" & "a fine mist" *a frayed red thread: tanka love poems* (Clinging Vine Press, 2001); "recovering from migraine" *AT* #8; "wildly flowing no more" *AT* #7; "paint me blurred" *Hummingbird* XII:4; "after that stormy night" *ridge whisperings beauty springs forth* (Universal Peace Press, 2001); "after mother's death" *bottle rockets* III:2. **Welch**: "this is but a moonless night" *Poetry Kanto* #17); "all my books collect dust" *TS* 1992; "the way you look at me" *TS* 2001; "jingle of the dog's collar" *AT* #11; "doing laundry" *TS* 1993; "her plane disappears" *Hummingbird* X:2 ; "a book on Hiroshima" *PR* #12; "two cars backing up" *TSA Newsletter* III:3; "freeway empty" and "you would not sleep on the pillow" *Countless Leaves*; "I tell her I grow old" *WN* #21; "my pen poised" *AT* #8; "this cold lonely night" *WN* #16; "a snail has left" *WN* #17. **Williams, A.**: "words" *BS* X:4; "a ring" *PR* #12; "closing" *Tanka Splendor* Award 2000; "older now" *Castles in the Sand*. **Williams, P.**: "the alarm goes off" *AT* #9. **Witkin**: "into the reeds" *Brussels Sprout* XI:3; "in a curve of light" *FLD* Winter 1995. **Young**: "Taking a break" & "Moonlight" *Mariposa* #3; "New vines spread" *AT* #11; "Dying sea lion" *TH* #3.

annemekay 110
june mareau 116-119 wild iris
Doris Kasson 78,79,80
cattails 93
stream 107-1 McClintock
farmers mkt 163
knowing less 148
amaryllis 42
and 43
4 - 2+3
bittersweet 52
56-1, 57-2
66-67
70-71
77-3
85-3
88.89
92-95
99-3
XXVI - XXVIII
XXXIV
115-1+3
126-127
knowing-148
Pat Shelley 150-3
snail trail 159
muse 162
168-1
George Swede 170-5

Cat 182
L.J. Ward 186-9

Black Nogd ge 31

Gary Hay 54b

cwex''
definition XXV
XXX, XXXiii
pivot 71
byoka XXXvi